Also by Dr. Wayne

BOOKS

Everyday Wisdo
Getting in the Gap (incl
Gifts from Eyki
How to Get What You Really, Really, Really, Really want
It's Never Crowded Along the Extra Mile
Manifest Your Destiny
No More Holiday Blues
101 Ways to Transform Your Life (flip book)
The Power of Intention
Pulling Your Own Strings
Real Magic
The Sky's the Limit
Staying on the Path
10 Secrets for Success and Inner Peace
What Do You Really Want for Your Children?
Wisdom of the Ages
You'll See It When You Believe It
Your Erroneous Zones
Your Sacred Self

AUDIO PROGRAMS

The Awakened Life
Choosing Your Own Greatness
Everyday Wisdom (audio book)
Freedom Through Higher Awareness
How to Be a No-Limit Person
It's Never Crowded Along the Extra Mile
The Keys to Higher Awareness
101 Ways to Transform Your Life (audio book)
The Power of Intention
A Promise Is a Promise (audio book)
Secrets of Your Own Healing Power
There Is a Spiritual Solution to Every Problem
Transformation
The Universe Within You
Your Journey to Enlightenment (six-tape program)

MEDITATION AUDIO/CD

Meditations for Manifesting: Morning and Evening
Meditations to Literally Create Your Heart's Desire

VIDEOCASSETTES

Creating Real Magic in Your Life
How to Be a No-Limit Person
The Miracle Mindset
What Do You Really Want for Your Children?

CALENDARS

Everyday Wisdom Flip Calendar

All of the above are available at your local bookstore, or may be ordered by visiting:
Hay House USA: **www.hayhouse.com**
Hay House Australia: **www.hayhouse.com.au**
Hay House UK: **www.hayhouse.co.uk**
Hay House South Africa: **orders@psdprom.co.za**

A Promise Is a Promise

An Almost Unbelievable Story
of a Mother's Unconditional Love
and What It Can Teach Us

Dr. Wayne W. Dyer

with Marcelene Dyer

HAY HOUSE, INC.
Carlsbad, California
London • Sydney • Johannesburg
Vancouver • Hong Kong

Published and distributed in the United States by: Hay House, Inc., P.O. Box 5100, Carlsbad, CA 92018-5100 • *Phone:* (760) 431-7695 or (800) 654-5126 • *Fax:* (760) 431-6948 or (800) 650-5115 • www.hayhouse.com • **Published and distributed in Australia by:** Hay House Australia Ltd., 18/36 Ralph St., Alexandria NSW 2015 • *Phone:* 612-9669-4299 • *Fax:* 612-9669-4144 • www.hayhouse.com.au • **Published and distributed in the United Kingdom by:** Hay House UK, Ltd. • Unit 202, Canalot Studios • 222 Kensal Rd., London W10 5BN • *Phone:* 44-20-8962-1230 • *Fax:* 44-20-8962-1239 • www.hayhouse.co.uk • **Published and distributed in the Republic of South Africa by:** Hay House SA (Pty), Ltd., P.O. Box 990, Witkoppen 2068 • *Phone/Fax:* 2711-7012233 • orders@psdprom.co.za • **Distributed in Canada by:** Raincoast • 9050 Shaughnessy St., Vancouver, B.C. V6P 6E5 • *Phone:* (604) 323-7100 • *Fax:* (604) 323-2600

Library of Congress Cataloging-in-Publication Data

Dyer, Wayne W.
    A promise is a promise :   An almost unbelievable story of a mother's unconditional love and what it can teach us / Wayne W. Dyer with Marcelene Dyer.
      p.   cm.
    ISBN 1-56170-348-6 (hardcover) • 1-56170-872-0 (tradepaper)
    1. O'Bara, Kaye. 2. Caregivers—Florida—Biography. 3. Coma-Patients—Home care. 4. Love. 5. Mothers and daughters.
I. Dyer, Marcelene. II. Title.
RB150.C60223   1996
362.1'9684—dc20
[B]

                96-9125
                CIP

ISBN 1-56170-872-0

06 05 04 03   13 12 11 10
1st Printing, August 1996
10th Printing, October 2003

Printed in the United States of America

⚜ ⚜ ⚜

This book is dedicated in awe to:
The Holy Family,

to:
One of God's holy families, the O'Baras
(Joe, Kaye, Edwarda, Colleen, and Ricky),

and to:
A saint with a stethoscope,
Louis Chaykin, M.D.

⚜ ⚜ ⚜

Contents

Introduction
by Wayne W. Dyer

I have read many definitions of love. My favorite by far is quite simple: "... Love is the art of giving. It asks nothing in return." Using this as my working definition, you are about to read an authentic love story.

This is not a novel with characters who fall in love in a romantic fashion. This is not a story with a plot that winds its way through literary channels to a clever conclusion. What you hold in your hand is a book about unconditional love. Each page represents a real-life, day-to-day commitment to giving and serving in the highest sense of love that I can imagine.

I have made no effort to follow any rules of literary presentation. I did not resort to any "filler" material to lengthen the manuscript or to engage the reader in extraneous details of this remarkable story.

What I have done is to relate, as directly and simply as possible, the story of a level of giving to another human being that is unknown to most of us. It is my impression that when the art of giving becomes absolutely unconditional, as it is with Kaye O'Bara, we will come to know the meaning of this quotation from A *Course in Miracles*: "If you knew who walks beside you on the way that you have chosen, fear would be impossible."

I place the emphasis on the word *knew*. To know is to have the direct experience and to have banished all doubt. Kaye knows that she is not alone. She knows that her daughter is also participating in the way that she has chosen. This knowing has permitted Kaye to serve unconditionally for over a quarter of a century, and it has made visible the divine intervention of the Holy Family.

But even more than this is the fact that all of us who read of Kaye's devotion and unflappable service are enriched immeasurably.

In the context of love being the art of giving and asking nothing in return, we are all assured that this kind of love is not just for fiction writers or reserved for those who have been deified. This kind of love is here and now. It is taking place among us, while the rest of us go about the business of our daily lives.

The story of Kaye and Edwarda O'Bara is indeed a love story that transcends our own experiences of love. It reminds us to look within and see where we can give unconditionally.

I have written this book to fulfill my own commitment to giving unconditionally in my own life. Furthermore, it is my intention to introduce you to these divine people through the pages of this book, while simultaneously providing you with some insights on what you can learn from becoming aware of this story. And finally, it is my intention to remove the onus of debt that has choked at the life force of the O'Baras for this past quarter of a century, by having the royalties go directly to Kaye and Edwarda.

As you read this short book, be aware of the power of your prayers, as well as your compassion in helping out these sacred souls. As you extend this compassion toward the O'Baras, remember to do the same for everyone on our planet as well. This, to me, is the lesson of Edwarda's long silence—to teach all of us to extend love unconditionally in every corner of our world, and to do it without asking anything for ourselves in return. Perhaps as the world takes on this challenge, Edwarda's role as a victim soul will become complete. I pray it is so.

In love and light,
Dr. Wayne W. Dyer

Introduction
by Marcelene Dyer

Edwarda, I want to thank you for your selflessness. I believe that you have suffered greatly. You are inside a body that is asleep. You have endured this state for over 26 years, and while I have lived my life fully, you, my dear friend, have sacrificed all of what I have experienced in order to be our teacher. Although I send you my deepest love, and I talk to you often throughout my day, nothing I can do can repay you for your gift to me. Shall I tell you of those gifts? I want to very much.

Love is first. When I entered your room, I felt a great love. Total acceptance of me. You looked deep into my eyes with a penetrating gaze. I felt a connection. An acknowledgment. It was timeless and sacred. Thank you.

Your mother is second. Thank you for sharing your mother with the world. To me, she is saintly. Your relationship prior to the journey of this coma was established in a foundation of mutual respect, under-standing, happiness, and deep, deep love. This permeates the rooms of your home.

Mother's Day is always special to me and, personally, I believe our mothers give us our first understanding of what it is to be loved. They are our teachers, surely, but also, our mother's love is our first or our closest connection to the love of God. My mother has always been there for me. As I mature, I realize this is my feeling of God, too. He is always there for me.

I believe our deepest need is to find the look of love beaming back at us. As long as we feel this, we are better able to love ourselves and others. Your mother, Kaye, shines *only* love when she speaks of you or sits beside you and holds your hand. Those moments of communion touch us all. Thank you.

Third, your sister, Colleen, who looked up to you with great adora-tion because, in her eyes, you could do no wrong, said to us, "Even though I messed up, my sister never judged me. She never looked dis-approvingly at me. I know she loves me." Colleen gave us a glimpse of her courage and her own faith that you have a divine purpose.

Edwarda, I thank you most profoundly for your gift to the world, for others like you whose bodies are not working perfectly. You have opened the window for them to receive. Hopefully, after your story has been told, no one will miss the opportunity to serve the spirit of the human being and look past the imperfections of our packaging.

A most humble thank you, I say to you, Edwarda, my friend. I am forever indebted to you as my most sacred teacher.

I love you,
Marcelene Dyer

Chapter One
Kaye

❧ ❧ ❧

"All my life I wanted to get married, have two girls to sew for, be 50, and have gray hair. In 1948, I started on this dream by marrying Joe. I succeeded in it all. God gave me a wonderful husband and then two girls in Edwarda and Colleen. We had a loving, caring life for 22 years. Then my angel, Edwarda, got sick and fell into a coma. We all decided, as a family, that she would come home if she wasn't fully recovered. We have never wavered in that decision, even after Dad died.

"God has given me the strength to care for Edwarda by sending angels in many forms—friends, families, strangers who became friends, and many others. God has given me the gift of staying cheerful and being able to help others. He has brought my daughter Colleen back to us to live, and she and the gift God gave her, a son named Ricky, have made the family complete.

"I'm doing what I think I should do, because all I ever wanted in life was to have two girls. God was very good and granted me my wish. So, if He gave me what I wanted, then I feel I should care for Edwarda until He is ready to either heal her, or take her to heaven."

— Kaye O'Bara

❧ ❧ ❧

1

It was the day after Christmas, 1995, when I (Wayne Dyer) read a story in the newspaper that was to have an immense effect on me, not only in the moments that it took to read the story, but for the rest of my life. The story was titled, "Her 25th Christmas in a Coma." It gave a brief synopsis of a mother who had been totally devoted to her comatose daughter for over a quarter of a century.

I have written about the need for unconditional love in our relationships, and I feel that my wife Marcelene and I, both as individuals and as parents, have contributed a great deal of unconditional love over the years. But this story of Kaye O'Bara surpassed anything that we had ever personally encountered. In fact, I was so attracted to this story that I read it aloud to Tracy, my oldest daughter, and Marcelene, commenting on what a phenomenally powerful person this woman must be.

Something in that newspaper account touched my soul in a way that it had never been touched before. Little was I to know that Kaye O'Bara and her daughter, Edwarda, who has been "sleeping" since the third day of January, 1970, were going to become an integral part of our lives.

Those of you who are familiar with my writing know that I believe that there are no accidents in our universe. Every single meeting and event in our lives is in some way orchestrated by a divine force or universal intelligence that flows through all things. The low points in our lives occur to teach us to generate the energy to propel ourselves to higher levels, and "strangers" to whom we are drawn or attracted have something to teach us, or vice versa. When there is a powerful inner knowing felt within one's being, it is a kind of intuition that is a nudge from the divine source. Ignoring these inner callings is the same as walking away from the path of higher awareness.

With the story of Kaye O'Bara, I was touched deeply. In fact, I was so moved that I wrote her a brief letter saying, "You are my hero," and sent her an autographed copy of a book I wrote some years ago called *Real Magic*, which explores the idea of being able to create miracles in our everyday lives. On my way to the post office, I kept thinking about the details of this woman's life. She seemed profoundly spiritual to me—a modern-day Mother Teresa right here in South Florida, only a few miles from where I lived. I mailed the package, still deeply in awe of this remarkable tale of absolute unconditional love in action.

Try to Imagine Just for a Moment...

Just for a moment, go back over the past quarter of a century. Twenty-five years! Imagine never once going to a movie or even taking a brief vacation. Imagine never going on a shopping trip for yourself, and never being able to go for a walk that lasts longer than a few minutes. Imagine never being able to leave your home for more than an hour or so for the entire 25 years because you had someone that you were committed to serving, loving, and literally keeping alive.

Just imagine never having the time to be sick for 25 years, with the exception of a 10-day period in which you were hospitalized for a heart attack, and then having to rush out of your own treatment to get back to your primary mission in life—taking care of someone else, despite your own need for rest and recuperation. Imagine in that time period losing your life partner to a massive heart attack, and then having your only other daughter get lost in a world of drugs and prison for some of those years. Imagine having to borrow, beg, and pray each day for the money to take care of the burgeoning medical expenses without the benefit of any insurance. Imagine those medical expenses being *four times* more than your meager income from Social Security.

Imagine that during all of these years, your child, who was a normal and creatively alive 16-year-old girl one day, and the next was in a coma, unable to move or communicate, needed to be fed every 2 hours, 24 hours a day (that's 12 times a day, every day for over a quarter of a century). And, in addition, imagine that she needed to have her blood checked and tested every four hours and be given an insulin injection (that's six times a day for over a quarter of a century). And, during this entire time period, try to imagine never sleeping for more than 90 minutes at a time, and being willing to sleep in a chair right next to your loved one. *Imagine*—25 years of your life without having the benefit of sleeping in a bed!

This is Kaye, yet this only scratches the surface of the depth of spirit in this remarkable woman and her equally remarkable daughter, Edwarda.

There is much for all of us to learn from this story. It goes way beyond the surface facts of a mother caring for her comatose daughter. When 16-year-old Edwarda slipped into a coma on the third day of

January, 1970, the last conversation she had with her mother before entering her long sleep went precisely like this:

"Promise you won't leave me, will you, Mommy?"

"Of course not. I would never leave you, darling, I promise. And a promise is a promise!"

As Kaye related that poignant moment to me, she added almost as an afterthought that she believed that Edwarda had a subconscious inkling that she was going to be leaving the world of waking consciousness for a long while—perhaps that she had even made an "agreement" to do so.

"You know, it was very strange," Kaye recollected. "She always called me Mom or Mother, but at that time, she said, 'You won't leave me, will you, Mommy?'"

        ✤   ✤   ✤

As I mailed the package off to Kaye, I said a silent prayer for her, and then proceeded to go about the business of my own life. I had rented an apartment on the west coast of Florida for a two-month period during which I would be commuting to my home while writing a new book on manifesting. My attention was now focused on this new project, and I thought about Kaye O'Bara only now and then, remembering her in my prayers and my manifestation meditations.

One evening after a long day of writing and researching, I turned on the television to watch the evening news. I was not paying much attention to the broadcast since I was busy preparing my dinner, but then I noticed that *Inside Edition* with Deborah Norville had come on after the news. I had been interviewed by Deborah several years back, and I recalled how enjoyable the radio interview had been. Deborah was a concerned mother as well as a working professional woman. She reminded me of my wife, who was also figuring out a way to combine both of these inner longings.

Deborah announced that *Inside Edition* would be featuring a story about a woman who had been taking care of her comatose daughter for 26-plus years, and they showed Kaye O'Bara reading to her daughter from *Real Magic*, the book I had just sent her. I had one of those synchronistic awarenesses that caused goose bumps and shivers to run throughout my body as Kaye read the opening line from my book: "This is a book about miracles."

Here I was, watching television, which I rarely did; seeing a show that I had never seen, and there was Kaye O'Bara reading to Edwarda from a book I had recently sent because I was so deeply touched by this woman's unconditional love toward her daughter. To top it off, the chapter title I was writing in my new book seemed to be smiling at me from its place in my old portable typewriter: "Connecting to the Divine Source with Unconditional Love." It was an overpowering moment. I watched the show and vowed to look up Kaye's address when I returned to my writing sojourn.

When I completed the book the following month, I arrived home to find a mound of correspondence waiting for me. The first letter I opened was a thank-you note from Kaye. I immediately called her, and she invited Marcelene and me to visit Edwarda in North Miami at our convenience. This was the beginning of a relationship that introduced me to the world of miracles and unconditional love on a level that I had only read and written about up until this time.

When we entered Kaye's modest little home, we were greeted by a woman who was full of life and devoid of self-pity. Her focus was exclusively on her daughter's well-being. She had devoted over 25 years to caring for her child, and in the process had forgotten how to be self-absorbed.

As we entered the room where Edwarda was resting, Marcelene and I both felt an immediate sense of peaceful energy that infused the room with love and gentleness. This seemed to be a sacred place, and we both commented, on our way home, that it felt similar to our experience at the chapel in Assisi. We had journeyed to Italy and the little chapel where St. Francis had conducted his services and had died in the 13th century. The divine sort of presence we encountered in that chapel was what we had both felt in Edwarda's room.

I had a feeling as I talked to Edwarda and held her hand that she was listening to me. I felt that in some mysterious way, she was responsible for our presence in that room, and that Kaye had played a key role in getting us there. I knew that Edwarda was connecting with me in some way that I could not elaborate or explain. Both Marcelene and I felt that we were making a conscious connection.

After an hour or so had passed, and we told Kaye that we were leaving, a small tear came to Edwarda's eye, and she appeared restless and agitated. Kaye immediately told Edwarda that we would be back, and her daughter seemed to return to her more restful posture.

This was the beginning of a growing love relationship between our family and the O'Baras. We began to visit every few days, bringing anything that we could to help out.

Kaye had been faced with enormous expenses over the years, and she was living under a mountain of debt that tugged almost violently at her fragile heart. She borrowed to the maximum on many credit cards, and then she would get more credit cards to pay off the old credit-card debts. She mortgaged and remortgaged her home many times, and she took out bank loans and borrowed from anyone willing to help. Over the years, she conducted charity auctions, and urged newspaper reporters to tell her story to help elicit funds to pay for the ever-expanding expenses for food, medicine, and health care for her daughter.

Dr. Louis Chaykin, Edwarda's doctor, was an angel, treating her for years without taking a cent for his services. While other expenses mounted, Kaye, with Dr. Chaykin's help, managed to keep Edwarda in the best possible health under the circumstances. Kaye's attitude and the reality of the situation are best described in Kaye's words:

> I figure that it costs over $3,000 a month to keep the house going. We keep the air conditioning on year round. It keeps the germs out. Edwarda's baby food runs $9 per day, and my drugstore bill for her medicine is over $1,000 a month.
>
> There was a time when I had 32 credit cards. No matter what she needed, I'd borrow it. Her nurse was $42 a day, and when you don't have that coming in, it adds up fast.
>
> I had to do this behind my husband's back while he was still alive because he couldn't take the strain. But I always knew that Edwarda's care came first and that God would help me to figure out a way to take care of the money issue.

When I heard this, I knew that there was one thing I could do. I could help Kaye remove this burden of debt from her life. I made a commitment to write this book and to have all the royalties paid direct-ly to the Edwarda O'Bara Fund. I could tell this story to the world and receive a triple bonus in the process.

First of all, I would help alleviate the strain of enormous debt and allow Kaye to turn her attention exclusively to getting Edwarda the care she required. A second benefit is how this story will affect readers. I believe that it will help others reach into their hearts and extend com-passion and love, which our world sorely needs. The third aspect is for my personal growth. For the first time in my life, I can turn all of my writing energy into something that will benefit another human being without bringing any financial remuneration to myself. I have the opportunity to replace my ego's interest with concern for others. As I write this book, I feel blessed in a multitude of ways, and I feel that Kaye is responsible for the feeling of grace that I am experiencing in connection with this commitment.

After several weeks of visiting with Kaye and Edwarda, I made a trip to Los Angeles to tape a television show. Marcelene called me while I was out there to tell me that I should make a special effort to see Kaye the following day, as Kaye had asked that I be at her home when the *Oprah* show was scheduled to interview her. I agreed, and was able to get on an all-nighter from Los Angeles to Miami.

When I arrived at Kaye and Edwarda's home, Oprah Winfrey's staff was filming the visitors throughout the day. I talked to Edwarda as I was now accustomed to doing, and I said a few words for the show, which aired a few days later.

Several people who had been involved with comas appeared on that particular *Oprah* show. The feature story was about a policeman who had been in a coma for eight or nine years and who had suddenly started talking. In addition, there were people on the show who had been in comas for shorter periods of time and who had returned to a waking state. The emphasis seemed to be on how difficult it was for friends and relatives who had witnessed their loved ones in a coma, and the struggle of their return to waking consciousness.

The doctors who were interviewed did not want to discuss the pos-sibility of miracles. They preferred to give a pessimistic, scientific explanation of what life in a coma does to the victim as well as the loved ones. The families seemed to be in a state of despair over their inability to communicate with their newly awakened loved ones and the "damage" that had occurred as a result of the comatose state. Everyone on the show shared a frustration over how the comatose state had adversely affected their lives—that is, until Kaye O'Bara, the last featured guest.

Here was a woman who had been caring for her comatose daughter for two-and-a-half decades, and she was upbeat, positive, and full of hope as she spoke. "It is my privilege to be able to serve in this way," she said. "God doesn't give you anything that you can't handle. I am honored to be of service. I know that Edwarda is there, that she is not that body that is dysfunctional temporarily, and that she is a divine soul who will wake up some day."

When I asked Kaye how she reacted to that show and all of the pessimism that she heard, her response was:

> I would love to call Oprah and get the address of the doctor. I think he crushed a lot of people's dreams. But he didn't crush mine. I think he is too scientific. I mean, science has its place, but God gives science knowledge. That's right—and you have to realize that God can do anything He wants. Even the brain of that scientist came from God. I don't want to think bad of the man, but he broke the dream of that guy on the show, and a lot of people were watching. As I sat and watched, I thought my heart was crushed for him, but he didn't crush my dream.

Kaye O'Bara was the highlight of that show. I was privileged to make a brief appearance with her and Edwarda to put the focus where I believed it ought to be. This remarkable woman and her equally remarkable daughter had shown us a side to unconditional love that most of us cannot even imagine. Kaye showed the world that day that despite what scientific prognostication says about a woman in a coma for so many years, her faith and belief in being positive and viewing her life circumstances as a gift from God is very much alive.

Kaye has an unshakable internal knowing that Edwarda will come out of her diabetic coma and that there is a spiritual lesson in this long saga in which she is participating. Her faith gives her the strength to serve without a moment's concern about her own personal struggles.

She thinks like a saint. She gives of herself tirelessly in the name of unconditional love. She has taught me and shown me first hand what it is like to tame the ego completely and to live in the pain and bliss of serving.

This is something that I have written about and something I have worked at achieving. But in all honesty, it is not something that I have come close to accomplishing when I see how it works in this woman. And now, she has given me this great gift of the opportunity to write for someone else...the gift to speak without thinking about how it will affect me...the gift to be able to serve unconditionally.

In Kaye's mind, this is the lesson of Edwarda's long sleep. We have the opportunity to learn about a new kind of compassion and to help spread it throughout the world. This is Edwarda's holy mission, according to Kaye, and the spiritual guidance that she has been given by the Blessed Mother (which you will read about in the third chapter). I am grateful to be a participant and to give you a book describing unconditional love in action.

Kaye O'Bara has been challenged and has met that challenge for a large portion of her adult life with nothing but awe and love in her heart. Her story is worth knowing and remembering. It can teach us all a great lesson in a multitude of ways.

❧   ❧   ❧

Kaye is the former Kathryn McCloskey whose father, Eddie, was the mayor of Johnstown, Pennsylvania. She was destined to become a care giver early in her life. Her mother died at the age of 58, and Kaye and her father took care of her right up to and including her passing.

Kaye's husband, Joe O'Bara, was a football star at the University of Pittsburgh and a boxing champion in the Navy. Two years after Edwarda lapsed into her coma, Joe had a massive heart attack, and Edwarda's total care became Kaye's responsibility. Joe was unable to do anything that required heavy lifting. Essentially, he was relegated to a position of observing his daughter in her comatose state. His heart was heavy, and it finally broke completely when he died four years later.

While interviewing Colleen, Edwarda's younger sister by 18 months, I learned the circumstances of their father's death. Colleen recalled, "I remember before my dad died—and this is what still keeps me going—he said, 'If they take me, darling, I am going to heaven to find out what I can do from there. Remember one thing, Colleen. If I don't take your sister with me, there's a reason for it, and one day she will wake up.'"

Joe also told Kaye a few days before he died, "I can't help Edwarda any more down here. I'm going to go up to heaven, and I'm going to help her from there. But don't you ever get depressed and think she won't wake up, 'cause she will."

After Joe died, it took Kaye six years before she was able to cry and grieve. During all of those years, her focus was on taking care of Edwarda. The strain had proved too much for Joe. He left almost nothing in his will. All of their finances and insurance had been eaten up by medical expenses.

The strain was evident on Kaye for a period of time as well. "I had a heart attack and fell onto Edwarda's bed on Mother's Day of 1982," she recalls. The ten days she then spent recuperating in a hospital were the only days that she has ever spent away from Edwarda's side. Her teaching career ended the day that she brought Edwarda home from the hospital in May of 1970. She has seen her mother pass away, as well as her beloved Joe, who could no longer stand the pain of seeing his daughter require so much attention while being unable to provide adequate financial help.

Joe wrote a letter to his two daughters just prior to his death. I've included a short excerpt of that letter, which reveals his anguish:

> Edwarda,
>
> I just can't find the words to tell you how much I love you. You mean so much to your daddy. I'm just sorry for not being a daddy, as a daddy should be. I just wish that God could find it to give you back your health. I want to hold you in my arms and tell you that you are the sweetest darling in the world.
>
> Colleen, I love you so. I'm sorry I haven't told you more often how much I love you. You and Edwarda are very precious to me.
>
> I am so sorry that I hurt your feelings when you were a little girl, Edwarda, without cause. I'm so very sorry. I ask God to give your daddy another chance to make up to you for all the wrongs

> *that I have done. You are both God's children. Forgive your daddy*
> *for ever being unkind to you, and know that I love you more than*
> *life. My love for you is more than my heart could ever speak. I love*
> *you and Colleen very much. God will always be with you, honey.*
> *I love you.*
> *Daddy.*

Colleen was very close to her father, while Edwarda was closest to her mom. Joe's death was more than Colleen could handle. She described her feelings at that time:

> *My dad died, and I had my son eight days later. And then I*
> *got lost. I was so lost that I didn't know what to do, and I was so*
> *lonely for my father that I took to drugs. I was almost in a coma*
> *like Edwarda. My mom was taking care of Ricky for me, and I*
> *still didn't know that I wasn't being a mom. It was like being out*
> *there, but I felt totally lost inside.*

For a long period of time, Colleen wavered back and forth between being at home for her son and then being out on the street living on drugs. Ultimately, she was arrested and spent a short period of time incarcerated. It was here that she found new strength and returned home to be with Kaye and Ricky. She knows about the love for a child, which she observed directly from Kaye.

"I know that my mom would do anything for me, anything, even though we sometimes argue and disagree. I know that she would die for me. That's just my mom," Colleen said.

Kaye took on the additional challenge of taking care of her grandson and the pain of knowing that Colleen was in her own waking coma, high and out of touch, and then in and out of the world of the street. Kaye's heart ached for both her daughters, while the daily responsibilities of caring for Edwarda every two hours around the clock, and attempting to come up with some plan to finance the growing indebtedness, plagued her.

The essential Kaye O'Bara is a woman who has lost her self-absorption, tamed her own ego, and turned her life over to the service of those she loves. She has been tested over and over, and she remains a positive role model for all of us. Her modest home is full of the love that she has radiated to her children all of these lonely, trying years.

That love is evident in Edwarda's appearance. She is sparkling clean, her gray hair braided, and her clothing always crisp and feminine. The care that has to go into making sure that Edwarda is always fresh and clean invites one to try to imagine Kaye's routine.

There is a chair by Edwarda's bedside, where one can only visualize the number of nights over a quarter of a century when Kaye has fed Edwarda: waking at midnight, 2:00, 4:00, 6:00, and 8:00 A.M., to pour the specially prepared baby food and vitamins into the feeding tube that is her daughter's life support. After the food, Kaye gently pours in water, then takes her place alongside Edwarda to suction out any phlegm that might be caught in Edwarda's throat. She will not tolerate any discomfort for her precious angel.

Kaye has a special, symbiotic relationship with Edwarda. She intuitively knows what is needed, and she keeps up a constant stream of conversation with her. She will play her positive self-help tapes, read to her from books about miracles, turn on the television when her favorite programs come on, and play meditation tapes and prayers for her. All of the time, she is also tracking Edwarda's progress.

Edwarda has her menstrual cycle every 28 days like clockwork, which is unusual for someone in a coma. When she is cramping, she is able to let her mother know, and Kaye then administers medication to relieve her pain. She can move her eyes across the room, smile in recognition, and cry in despair.

Over the years, Edwarda has moved from being in a deep coma to being able to blink her eyes in response to a question from Kaye. When an unfeeling visitor once remarked that Edwarda was a vegetable, Kaye immediately responded that she'd never seen a vegetable smile.

Kaye shaves Edwarda's legs and bathes her daily, explaining, "Everything goes on, but she is just not talking and not walking. And remember, in over 26 years, she has never had a bedsore."

This, of course, reflects Kaye's determination that Edwarda's body will be moved around and will always be made comfortable, regardless of how much work is involved. She will not permit bars to be placed on her bed for fear that it might make Edwarda think she is back in the hospital, where she experienced terrible pain back in 1970. Moreover, no one is allowed to wear white in Edwarda's room because it might make her think that the person is a nurse. Kaye is taking no chances that Edwarda might think she is back in a hospital setting. At all times, Kaye thinks of her daughter and what might be going on inside her. She keeps track of the little improvements that tell her that Edwarda will one day awaken.

"One day," Kaye says confidently, "she will reveal what transpired and tell us beautiful things about heaven. She will bring people back to God through her miracle awakening. And if God takes me, He'll have to make her better or take her with me. I trust completely that He will do what is best."

But while Kaye is here with Edwarda, hope never even comes close to dying. Edwarda murmurs and smiles and occasionally reacts to the television set. She moves her head now, whereas once this was impossible. She opens and closes her eyes now, whereas once they had to be taped in order to close them. Kaye watches and observes every change in her daughter.

Kaye has been asked many times why she didn't allow Edwarda to go to a nursing home, where the government would have taken care of her expenses, and life would have been much easier for Kaye. Her response was immediate and forthright:

"I knew she would never survive long in a nursing home, and so did my husband. I made her a promise that I would never leave her, and once you make a promise, you are morally and spiritually obliged to live up to it. I know she will wake up one day. I will be here just like I was on the 3rd of January in 1970, and she will know that I lived up to that promise that I made when she was just a little girl. You know, Doc," Kaye said, looking at me through those beautiful, tired gray eyes, "a promise is a promise!"

I know what she means.

What We Can Learn from Kaye and How We Can Apply It

There are five important lessons that I have gleaned from my association with Kaye O'Bara. I suggest that you consider them as you continue reading this miraculous saga. You may want to apply these lessons in your own life. When Kaye knows that her struggles have benefited others in any small way, she feels that all of the struggle has been worth it and that she and Edwarda have been doing God's work.

1. *Unconditional love means without conditions.* Love the significant people in your life in a way that asks for nothing in return. Do not ask to be thanked or rewarded in any way. Simply serve, and give your love as Kaye has done over these past 26 years.

   This unconditional approach has many built-in rewards, but essentially it is the very force that keeps us attuned to our higher selves. When we tame the ego and reach out without conditions, our lives are enriched immeasurably.

2. *Put your own troubles into perspective.* In the light of the daily load that Kaye has assumed, most of your own troubles pale in significance. When you are distracted, angry, hurt, or full of self-pity, bring the image of Kaye into your consciousness, and notice how your "troubles" diminish in importance.

   It is the ego that causes you to view your problems as situations that may overwhelm you. When you tame the ego by thinking of how lucky you are in contrast with those who have much greater burdens, you tune into your spiritual self. It is this sacred self that will bring you peace.

3. *Be generous.* Make a conscious effort to be generous by taking time to give of yourself and your resources to those in need.

Kaye has lived with indebtedness ever since she resigned her teaching position in 1970. She lives by the generosity of others and still has accumulated a mountain of debt. Yet she always practices generosity when it comes to dealing with others, particularly with her daughters. We have committed ourselves to helping Kaye remove debt from her life by writing this book for her and her family.

If you would like to help Kaye, even in a small way, you may contribute a tax-deductible donation to The Edwarda O'Bara Fund at the address at the end of this book. Kaye responds to every donation that she receives.

4. *Never give up hope.* This is the theme of Kaye O'Bara's life. Hope is one thing that Kaye clings to. She has a deep and abiding faith in God that has never been shattered, even for a moment. She knows that as long as Edwarda is alive, there is hope.

    Remove yourself from the influences of naysayers, and know within your heart that the universal law that has allowed any miracle to ever take place in the history of humanity has not been repealed. Miracles do occur. They are much more likely to occur when you keep your faith and refuse to give in to pessimism. Remind yourself that no one knows enough to be a pessimist.

5. *It is an honor to serve others.* This is the greatest lesson of Kaye's life. She sees herself as privileged to carry out this mission of service, regardless of how trying it has become. Adopt the attitude that Kaye demonstrates daily.

    Rather than feeling sorry for yourself and going through life with an attitude of pity, practice doing what you love and loving what you do in the service of others. Be thankful, as Kaye is, for being blessed in such a way. When you are given the opportunity to serve others and to let go of your own self-absorption, you will feel purposeful and peaceful.

Be in quiet commerce with God from a position of gratitude for the strength to serve anyone who requires your assistance. Think of Kaye, rarely sleeping, being on duty 24 hours a day for a quarter of century and never complaining or being angry. Remind yourself of Kaye's "theme song": "God never gives you something you can't handle."

Treat serving as an honor, and remove the pain and anguish from your life, replacing it with a heartfelt sense of unconditional love—the sort of love that gives you the strength to carry out your mission of service. Continually remind yourself that you are being honored in all of your service to others—and not being punished.

This is a brief synopsis of Kaye O'Bara's way of life. I could have written hundreds of pages on this remarkable woman and all that she has accomplished in her lifetime. I have chosen to keep it short and describe the basics of this saintly woman.

Now, I would like to introduce you to Edwarda.

Chapter Two
Edwarda

⚜   ⚜   ⚜

Dearest Edwarda,

You rest in the loving hands and heart of our Lord. We do not question His motives for your long earthly sleep, but bow only to His holy will. We place our trust in Him and know that our faith will be rewarded in His good time. Jesus loves you very much, and through you, many have come to know Christ and themselves better. Through your devoted mother's care for you, many of us have come to know the real meaning of sacrifice and love for one another.

In wishing you a very happy birthday, we beg our Lord to grant you your fondest wish, and His choicest blessings on you and your heroic mother.

May you find peace in the arms of Jesus.

— Fred
(A man well into his 90s who is a
devoted writer to Edwarda.)

⚜   ⚜   ⚜

17

After 26 years, the tendency is to think of Edwarda as the young girl who has grown into a woman while being in a coma. She has become labeled as the miracle woman who has survived all of these years against all odds while being in a state of sleep, and she's had stories written about her called "Edwarda's Long Journey" and, as I mentioned previously, "Her 25th Christmas in a Coma."

Writing about her this way is a natural tendency, since Edwarda's experience of being comatose for over a quarter of a century is mind-boggling, and when she awakens she will set a record that will be even more astonishing. But Edwarda is much more than the girl/woman who has remained comatose for so long. There is a deeply spiritual story here, and Edwarda is at the heart of this story.

There have been visits from the Blessed Mother, which I will recount in the following chapter. There are miracles taking place around this profoundly sacred woman, some of which I have related in the final chapter. Edwarda O'Bara has lived a life that can teach all of us something about applied spirituality.

I have spoken with the key people in Edwarda's life, and I have read everything that has been written about her. I have spent many hours talking to Edwarda and observing her mother doing the same. I have prayed with Edwarda, and I have observed her with Marcelene and our children. I have seen her respond. I have seen her smile. I have seen her cry, and I have looked directly into her eyes and seen her awareness of my presence.

I know that Edwarda is much more than a body in a coma. I know because I have witnessed first hand that Edwarda's mission is being accomplished right now in this very moment, despite her immobility, and despite what we label as her sickness. This is a divine being, fulfilling her mission, just as each and every one of us is doing, regardless of our physical-world limitations. Edwarda is a soul with a body, a body that remains still while she teaches all of us the great lessons that she came to teach.

Kaye has said to me many times, "It is my honor to take care of Edwarda. She is doing so much more than just lying in her bed than others who are able to walk around are accomplishing."

When you discover just what kind of person this beautiful soul is, both before she entered the silent, temporary state of light sleep, and since that day back in 1970, you will see divine qualities that are rarely observed in any of us.

Edwarda's is not a story of medical terminology. It is not a story of coma data and lingo, nor is it about the prognosis that medical experts provide concerning the stages of a coma. Edwarda's story transcends the material world and makes scientific predictions irrelevant. Edwarda is a rare, saintly person who has been this way since she arrived here on the 27th of March in 1953.

Early on, she possessed qualities that marked her for a heroic mission that was rooted in spirituality, rather than this material world of possessions and self-absorption. She personified the idea that we are not human beings having a spiritual experience, but that the reverse is more accurate: *we are spiritual beings having a human experience.* In all that I could find out about Edwarda, she seems to be first and foremost a spiritual being having a human experience. Her human experience is more attuned to those we describe as saintly or sacred.

This, then, is Edwarda's story. As you read about this remarkable girl, and about the role of the Blessed Mother, you will have a clearer picture of Edwarda—a picture that makes her comatose state a minor part of this astonishing story.

༺✿༻ ༺✿༻ ༺✿༻

Edwarda was a baby who always had a smile, according to Kaye. "She was happy and friendly with everybody. Later, as a toddler, she loved to sing and dance. She rarely, if ever, cried." Eighteen months after Edwarda's birth, her sister Colleen came into the family. "When I brought Colleen home from the hospital, Edwarda was completely thrilled. She only wanted to be with Colleen, to take care of her. They were absolutely inseparable," Kaye told me.

During those early years, Kaye was taking care of her sick mother, and she noted one key thing about Edwarda—her incredible *compassion.* That's a word that always came to mind when Kaye thought about her young daughter. Edwarda seemed to care deeply for everyone she encountered, and she showed an enormous amount of pathos for her grandmother, who was suffering with cancer. "I think that's where she got her compassion, when she was sitting with my mother and saw her so sick," Kaye recalled.

When Edwarda started school, Kaye began to notice that she was not at all like the other children when it came to this quality of compassion. Kaye illustrated this point with the following story:

> There was a little boy in her class who was slightly retarded. Others would say he was badly retarded. And there was also a handicapped little girl in the class. She went to them as soon as she started school and got to be friends with them. Some of the other kids would make fun of them. Edwarda wouldn't bother with the ones that made fun. It got to where those two were accepted throughout the school. She stayed friends with them right up until the ninth grade, and she made it a point to see that they were always included and accepted by everyone else.

Edwarda's story as a young girl is one of almost unbelievable service to others. She displayed Christlike qualities in virtually all of her encounters, and I did not hear anyone dispute this observation. Edwarda would stop what she was doing and assist people crossing the street if they had a cane. She babysat for the neighborhood children and refused to take money. It was her natural instinct to serve others.

Her sister, Colleen, was the more talented singer and dancer, so when they performed, Edwarda's reaction was always: "My sister can do this better than I can." It never bothered her for even a moment. She was proud of her sister. There was simply no rivalry because Edwarda was always so happy about the success of others. This was true in her relationships with virtually everyone. One particularly compelling story was related by both Kaye and Colleen:

"She was always good," Kaye told me, "almost beyond belief. One time she was up for an award in her class at school for being first in the class, and there was another little girl in the class who never received anything. She went to her teacher and said, 'She knows the material better than I do; she's just afraid to say it.'

"The teacher said, 'Well, she's second, Edwarda, but you're first.'

"'Can't I please refuse it so that Mary Lou can get the award?' Edwarda pleaded.

"The next day," Kaye continued, "the teacher announced to the class that Mary Lou was the one who was supposed to receive the award. It was the only award that this child ever got in grade or high school. Edwarda knew that it meant more to make Mary Lou happy than to have her own award."

This is the kind of child that Edwarda was during all of her school years. She displayed qualities that set her above the rest and was on a spiritual path without it being labeled that way.

When Edwarda saw other children her age drinking and smoking, she refused to judge them, but she felt compelled to help them. One time she asked Kaye if it was all right to go to the parents of a friend so she could help this girl without getting her into trouble.

"I guess you could call her a snitch," Kaye told me. "She tried first with the kids to get them to quit. Then if they wouldn't quit and she really knew the family well, she would go to her girlfriends' mothers. One time a mother was furious. 'Not my Ricky. She would never do drugs.' But when Edwarda told her, she immediately went to school officials and reported that her daughter was involved with drugs at school. She said, 'I never believed it until Edwarda O'Bara told me. I know that Edwarda never tells a lie.'"

In fact, Edwarda was a child throughout all of her waking years who was incapable of telling a lie. She would not exaggerate a truth. She seemed to innately know the value of honesty, and she lived that way.

Edwarda's compassion extended beyond her immediate family and school friends. She showed remarkable love for others, never faltering, regardless of how others treated her. If she had 20 cents in her pocket, she would automatically give it to someone who was begging, even if that money would have bought something she truly wanted. There was no middle ground for her.

If it was cold, she took an extra sweater with her to give to a street person. She would give away anything she had to anyone. It was her nature to be giving and to not think about herself. "Colleen would spend money when they went shopping because she knew that Edwarda would give her whatever she had left," Kaye explained.

Her compassion was evident when she and Colleen went to the stables. Colleen loved to ride horses, and Edwarda loved being around these animals. Edwarda seemed to be fearful of riding, but her primary interest at the stables was to help other people take care of their horses. Kaye described Colleen and Edwarda's visits to the stables:

> *Colleen would be out riding, but not Edwarda. She just wanted to help—whether it was to clean up the stables or to assist the younger children. When Colleen was getting a pony as a gift from her father, Edwarda only wanted to talk about Colleen's pony. All she was concerned about was that Colleen got her pony and got what she wanted. Joe thought that we should get Edwarda something. But Edwarda insisted that she was just happy that Colleen got her pony. After they picked up the mare, Colleen spent all her time riding the horse, and Edwarda spent all of her time cleaning and waiting.*

I asked Kaye if Edwarda ever gossiped about other kids, as all teenagers seem prone to do. Kaye adamantly replied, "Absolutely never. If someone would say something bad to her about someone else, she would stop it right there. She wouldn't let it go around. I never heard her talk about anybody. The kids all say they never heard her talk about anyone either. She never found fault with anyone." Kaye interrupted herself and called to Colleen to come into the room. As Colleen entered, Kaye asked her if she ever heard Edwarda say anything bad about other people.

Colleen didn't hesitate to affirm, " No, never. She wouldn't do that. She was always more concerned about others than herself. If someone hurt my sister, she would just let it go and walk away. I was the physical one. I always fought for my sister because she wouldn't do it herself. Once a kid knocked my sister down on a bicycle, and I grabbed the kid. All I knew was that he had hurt Edwarda, and that's all that mattered to me. I was beating him up bad, I was so mad. But Edwarda would just let things go."

Edwarda appears to be a child that was almost too good for this world—a child who was living the spiritual principles taught by all religions, and who seemed to be doing so without any prompting or instruction. She exhibited the qualities of spiritual consciousness from the very beginning.

As a youngster, Edwarda appeared to be fragile and frail. She was afraid to go on an escalator unless someone held her hand. She eschewed any and all arguments and fights. She never spoke unkindly about anyone. She always displayed a quality of love and tolerance for everyone she encountered. She was an excellent student, but avoided the spotlight. She seemed to know that it was not appearances that mattered in life, but substance. That must be why she would ask to have her name removed from the honor roll. It brought her unwanted attention.

Edwarda seems to be a child of peace and a great admirer of The Prince of Peace. Enlightenment has often been defined as being immersed in, and surrounded by, peace. In this sense, Edwarda is a highly evolved, enlightened being. She lived with, and hopefully currently lives with, an inner peace. She did everything that it was possible to do to avoid conflict and maintain peace. She brings peace to those who seek her comfort today as well.

Kaye told me, "If there was an argument taking place in the house, she would go into her room and cry. If anyone raised their voice at somebody else, she would cry. Even today, if Colleen and I have an argument, Edwarda shuts her eyes when we shout because she doesn't want to hear our voices."

Edwarda has always been a child of peace. It was crucial for her to help others to feel peaceful. Perhaps it is this sense of peace that she always surrounded herself with that plays a role in her comatose state today. This is how her sister, Colleen, thinks about her:

> It's just, I know my sister. I know that she's just not a fighter. She always just took things as they were, and she still does today. Like I said, she's in her own safe little world now. If I could put my hand on her and make her get up, I'd do it, because I'm a fighter, and Edwarda is not.
>
> She doesn't have the stamina to fight, or take a chance on not feeling that pain again if she wakes up. Me, I would take the chance. I'd say, okay, if it hurts, I can always go back in. That's the way I'd do it. But Edwarda always detested fighting.

Colleen's insights were very profound to me. Next to Kaye, she has always been the closest to Edwarda, taking on the role in their early years of being Edwarda's protector. Colleen knew how gentle, peaceful, and nonjudgmental her sister was, and she did not want others taking advantage of her, as they were apt to do in those school years.

Colleen talked candidly about her own years of being lost. She said that she would talk to her comatose sister, telling Edwarda that she, Colleen, was messing up. She said that she even envied Edwarda, whose comatose state seemed easier than Colleen's life on the streets and in the drug scene. After talking to Edwarda, Colleen said that she always felt peaceful, both before and after the coma, because Edwarda would never be judgmental.

This strikes me as one of the highest virtues that any of us can attain. I asked Colleen if Edwarda ever told on her when she smoked.

"No!" Colleen exclaimed. "When we went to school, I went across the street where everyone went to smoke in the bushes. Edwarda knew what I was doing, but she not only never told, she never made a comment."

I asked Colleen if she believed that Edwarda was aware of what was happening to her while she was lost and doing drugs in the street.

"Yes," she replied, "and I still would go in and talk to her, and I never saw a look of disappointment in her eyes where I was concerned. When I would talk to her about it, I'd say 'I don't know why I'm doing this.' Now, when she has a look of disgust, like if she's watching TV, I just get that feeling from her, that disgust. Never did I ever get that look or a disgusted attitude or the feeling that she thought less of me. She just understood, just accepted it."

"Even when she was unconscious?" I asked.

"Yes, she just accepted me like she always did, even though I know it conflicted with her own standards," Colleen answered.

"And you can never think of a time when, as her little sister, she ever judged you?" I asked.

"No, absolutely never. No matter what I ever did, she never judged me," Colleen insisted.

"How about someone in the news or on TV, like a murderer?" I wondered out loud.

Colleen seemed thoughtful for a moment and said softly, "She simply didn't comment. If she saw someone begging for money, she would give it to them, but she never judged them—or *anyone*."

This is a remarkable quality for anyone to have, let alone a young girl. Everyone that I spoke to reaffirmed this trait of Edwarda's. Cousins, aunts, friends—they all said the same thing: Edwarda never judged anyone.

Colleen is certain that Edwarda will one day awaken. When I asked her if she truly believes in her heart that Edwarda will wake up, she responded without a moment's hesitation. "One day, yes, I am positive. I see my dad. I believe anything my father ever told me, and he would have had it worked out with God that we didn't have to put my mom and sister through this if there wasn't a reason for her to get well in the end. I believe that when she wakes up, she is not going to have lost any time. I know that she understands what is going on and that she will awaken."

When I asked Colleen why she thought Edwarda was living her physical life this way and for what purpose, she gave me the following answer:

> Well, I used to say that people have drifted so far away from the Church that it's going to take a miracle to bring them back. But I don't think that anymore. I think that with my mom, people are beginning to show more compassion than they used to. I think that my sister's reason is to teach people to have more compassion. That is her mission, and she can fulfill it from her bed. She will awaken when she knows this is taking place. That's just my view.

There is much to think about in the views presented by Colleen. Edwarda's presence is indeed a peaceful, nonjudgmental one.

When Marcelene and I are alone with Edwarda, we sense a higher presence in the room. We agree that there is a spiritual reason for her continuing in this state for so many years and that Kaye's role in teaching all of us about unconditional love is spiritually inspired, also. I feel that my strong attraction to this family and their story somehow fits in with the higher purpose of Edwarda's comatose state. I know that telling her story causes people to generate more compassion and return to a more peaceful state of grace because I have spoken about Kaye and Edwarda in speeches around the country. Everyone seems to recognize a living example of someone who has exhibited the highest qualities of the most spiritual among us. All are touched by this person going into a mode of sleep to teach us compassion.

I am reminded somewhat of the story of Gandhi, who refused to eat and went into deep meditations as long as the people of his country were behaving with judgment or violence. When the populace could no longer collectively handle the facts of their master teacher suffering, somehow the violence was quelled. From a position of silence and inner sleep, a waking coma if you will, a great spiritual teacher was able to impact the consciousness of the world. I see the parallels here with Edwarda as well.

Kaye told me that Edwarda was obsessed with the lives of the saints when she was a young girl in Catholic school. She carried the biographies of saints with her everywhere she went.

"She loved St. Anne, St. Catherine, and St. Wilhelmina," Kaye explained, "but particularly she loved St. Theresa. She would read everything that she could about them. This started when she was in the second grade. She used to have a little book, and then she went into bigger books. She loved the Blessed Mother and prayed to her all the time. She often said that the saints gave her comfort and a sense of peace in her life."

The more I learned about Edwarda, the more I felt that this child possessed virtually all of the qualities for sainthood herself. She lived a peaceful life. She always forgave others; she never held grudges because she simply did not know how to judge any one or any thing. If she saw or heard something that she did not agree with, she would simply pass on it. If she saw pain, she would attempt to ease it. This quiet teenager, who caught the flu around Christmas of 1969, and then a few days later slipped into a painful diabetic coma, lived with us long enough to make a huge impact on the lives of those close to her.

Now, after a quarter of a century of silence, she speaks to us of compassion, peace, forgiveness, service, and unconditional love. Her story, which remained obscure for many years, is beginning to be known throughout the world. She is featured in newspaper stories and national television shows, and she has a book written about her and her extraordinary mother. People come to her from distant places, and they experience healing and increased peace in their lives.

Edwarda and Kaye have been instrumental in bringing my own family closer together. Our children have gone into the room with Edwarda and have sung to her. It is a joy to know that they care enough to sing. They notice her appreciation in the most subtle of ways that only children are capable of sensing. Our younger children hop right up on the bed and hold her hand. They bring her poetry and drawings, and most importantly, they include her in their prayers.

Marcelene and I have never left the O'Baras without marveling at the enormous amount of love that seems to be present there. We count our own blessings, and we are in awe of the commitment to love that radiates into every corner of that home and into us when we are blessed to be there.

We both believe that if enough people hear the message of Edwarda and Kaye, it will be like a small ripple extending outward to the rest of the world, sending a message of peace and compassion, which seems to be what both of these divine lives are all about. As this message circulates throughout the world, perhaps Edwarda will feel that her long sleep need not be further extended.

This is not in our hands. But we all know the enormous power of prayer and how healing it can be. We ask that all of you who are reading this story put Kaye, Edwarda, Colleen, and Ricky in your prayers. We ask that you yourself take on the qualities of love, nonjudgmentalness, peace, forgiveness, and gentleness as your own way of making this story complete.

Kaye and Edwarda's story is not complete, however, without your knowing about the visitations of the Blessed Mother.

The next chapter concerns itself with the visitations of the Blessed Mother to Edwarda's bedside. Edwarda has much in common with all that is spiritual in the teachings of Jesus Christ and other denominations and religious persuasions. In this next, rather unorthodox chapter, we learn some things from the Blessed Mother that make these parallels even more astounding.

I ask you to keep an open mind. I can relate to you without any reservations that being in the presence of Edwarda O'Bara and her mother, Kaye, brings us a renewed sense of healing and spiritual nurturance. You cannot help but be touched by the story of Edwarda's life.

Edwarda is living, breathing, and helping others find the sacred in all things. She can teach all of us many significant lessons. Following are a few of the more obvious ones that you may want to emphasize and work on in your own life each day.

What We Can Learn from Edwarda and How We Can Apply It

After studying the 43 years of Edwarda's life, there are five lessons that stand out. As we think about and pray for the recovery of this divine soul, we can benefit from learning and applying these lessons in our personal lives.

1. Be *appreciative of your loved ones in every present moment.* There are times in our lives when we tend to take our loved ones for granted. We forget how precious they are until they are hurt or taken away from us in some way. Be thankful for every moment, in the precious times that you have with your children.

    Be grateful for everything about them, in particular whatever aspects you may take for granted, such as their smiles, health, funny little habits, their thoughtfulness, and even the things that you find annoying. Stop in the middle of your outburst, and feel yourself smile. Think of Edwarda and all that inner beauty, and convey this message to your loved ones.

2. *We are not our bodies, we are souls with bodies.* Our inclination is to put our attention on what we can observe with our senses, and to treat only this as reality. But our bodies, like everything in the physical world, are simply like quiet bits of dust, parts of a process that is always changing and transforming the physical, material world into something else.

    The authentic self never changes. Some call this the perennial self. Acquaint yourself with the unfolding of God in everyone that you encounter, perhaps beginning with your loved ones. Relinquish an emphasis on appearance and accomplishment. Know that every one of us is a piece of God, deserving of love for this and no other reason.

    Edwarda's body is not walking around. Her limbs

temporarily lay at her sides, yet she is just as much an extension of God as any Olympic athlete. Try to see this in everyone, and you will erase any obsession with appearance and performance. The result will be more love and light for everyone.

3. *Become aware of the power of peace.* Often there is a tendency to resort to anger or physical manipulation to get a point across. We have all raised our voices and yelled at someone who was not doing our bidding the way we wanted it done. Some will speak of hating those who disagree with them or break the rules. And there are some who strike out with fists or slap those who are smaller and defenseless. Remove all traces of this habit of ego from your life by consulting your sacred self when those moments occur.

    You can make much more of an impact by being gracious and being unthreatening yourself, in the face of discord. You can remove judgment, as was Edwarda's way in her waking life. You can only give away what you have inside. If you are filled with rage, that is what will come out when you are pressured or squeezed in some way.

    Edwarda's life is a dramatic picture of the power of peace. You can remove inner rage by meditating on Edwarda and her profound peacefulness. Being at the mercy of those who annoy you is the same as turning your life over to those who are less peaceful than you. Put peace into your heart, and extend it in a nonjudgmental way, just as Edwarda has done throughout her life.

    The essence of spirituality is living peacefully and generating that peace wherever you are. Enlightenment is the state of being surrounded by, and immersed in, peace. I feel that Edwarda's long sleep is a metaphor for this idea of being in peace and sending it out to all whom we encounter.

4. *God is in everything and everyone.* Keep in mind that the universal life force that we know as God is omnipresent. God is not in some of us and absent in others. We do have the choice as to how we use this God force, but it is everywhere and in everyone. Learn to honor this awareness.

   Know that God is not a punishing force, but a force of unconditional love. We cannot understand why someone goes into a coma for so many years, but it is only our ego minds that fail to comprehend. God is working through each and every one of us. It is our minds and personalities that say it should be different than it is. God often works in ways that are incomprehensible to our intellects.

   We must honor this life force that is in each and every one of us, even though our ego minds say it is a tragedy, or that something is wrong. Nothing is wrong. Edwarda's life mission is on target. She is serving all of us, and therefore serving God, because God is in all of us. When she is to awaken, she will do so.

   Never doubt the life force that is in each and every thing and person. When this life force, what we call our life, leaves our body, there is no change in the weight of our physical body. Our lives are weightless. Our bodies weigh the same alive and dead. Our life is in a dimension that defies weights and measures. It is this formless, weightless, boundaryless, immeasurable aspect of ourselves that we know as the God force that we must always honor.

5. *As long as you are alive, your life mission is incomplete.* In his book, *Illusions*, Richard Bach wrote that there is a test to determine if your life's mission is complete. "If you are alive," he wrote, "it isn't." Know that each and every one of us has a heroic mission to accomplish. Every breath of your life is in the direction of this spiritual purpose.

Not all of us are here to be saints in the eyes of a religious authority, but we are all saintly in that we have the God force within us. Our bodies are nothing more than the curriculum that we are taking to reach God. If your body cannot see or hear, or is missing a limb, or immobilized, this is not an indication that your life mission is canceled.

You can do your work from a wheelchair as well as a pulpit...from a bed in a quiet room or from behind a piano. Edwarda is no less on target in her life mission because she does not talk to us or move around, nor is your purpose any less valid and important because of any of the physical circumstances of your life. Every breath that you take is a giving and a receiving of the life force that is your sacred self.

You take in a deep breath as a gift from this force, and you release it back into the air as your return gift. You will absolutely know when your life mission has been completed. At that moment, you will enter into a state of pure bliss, symbolizing your reunification with God. While those breaths continue to give and take, you are also participating in the mission that you signed up for when you entered your body at the moment of your conception.

This, then, is Edwarda—a divine, peaceful, nonjudgmental, unconditionally loving, forgiving, quiet child of God. She lays motionless and without words, but she gives all of us pause to consider the miraculousness of our own lives and how we might improve them by taking on some of these qualities that she possesses.

An Irish priest responded to Kaye's question of what use Edwarda's life could possibly be, by saying, "Truly she gives meaning to our lives."

And Kaye says, "I'm afraid someone will think I am crazy, but I believe she's doing the work of the Lord."

I can assure you that I know you are not crazy, Kaye. We are all working at allowing our higher sacred selves to triumph over our lower selves rooted here in the material world. You and Edwarda are way ahead of most of us.

Chapter Three
The Blessed Mother

"You suffer as you do for those whose hearts are full
of greed. The pain you endure in silence has won
many souls, through Jesus, my Son."

— Message from the Blessed Mother to Christina Gallagher,
Irish visionary and stigmatist, Monday, November 29, 1993

Edwarda O'Bara and her mother, Kaye, are profoundly spiritual people. Edwarda always wanted to know more about the Blessed Virgin Mary. The idea of the Blessed Mother providing guidance and light both for individuals and to an increasingly darkening world, mesmerized Edwarda.

As Kaye described earlier, Edwarda was constantly reading about the saints and the Blessed Mother, carrying books with her everywhere. Often she'd be seen avidly reading in her bedroom, and then she'd excitedly talk to Colleen and her mother about these saints who lived in the time of Christ. It was as if Edwarda felt that by learning more and more about the Blessed Mother and many of the female saints, she would be able to commune directly with them.

For Edwarda, this was very important business. She regarded her spiritual world very seriously, and she viewed the lives of the saints with reverence. She never seemed to feel that the spiritual life was being imposed on her.

Religion and spirituality are a central theme in this amazing story for both Kaye and Edwarda. This attitude is apparent in the following statement that Kaye made in a national religious publication:

> *When you get married, you dedicate your marriage to some-*
> *thing. Ours was dedicated to the Holy Family. Don't get me*
> *wrong—I'm not classifying myself with them. But we tried to pat-*
> *tern our life after the Holy Family. Every time I get down, I*
> *remind myself that Mary would never give in. I don't think I am*
> *exceptional.*

While Kaye dedicated her marriage to the Holy Family, young Edwarda worshiped the Blessed Mother and St. Anne. She did not preach to or judge others who did not revere these saints in the way she did. In fact, she would not even comment on disbelievers. Edwarda simply had an internal knowing for herself about the importance of these entities and how they could be relied upon in times of trouble.

I am certain that she received a great deal of her spiritual influence from her parents and her schooling, but I do not believe it is possible to inject this kind of an attitude into anyone who is not called on to receive it. Exposure is one thing, but making an internal commitment and living that commitment every day is quite another matter. Edwarda seemed to have a spiritual calling.

She was admitted to the first class at the University of Notre Dame that allowed females to register. She was excited about being accepted and looked forward to studying at such a sacred school as Notre Dame, particularly since she would be in the very first class that admitted young women. For her, this was a divine message from the Holy Family, and she felt that her life would be tremendously enriched by attending that fine institution.

But Edwarda's life took a different turn. No one could have predicted that she would slip into a comatose state for over 26 years. She was a mild diabetic, but nobody, including her medical caretakers, foresaw an occurrence of that magnitude.

What happened to Edwarda has never challenged Kaye's faith. When an interviewer with *The National Catholic Register* asked her about the redemptive value of suffering, which the Pope has written about, her response was:

> It may sound strange, but I don't feel I suffered. I still have
> Edwarda. But I do hope, because God is good, that there will be a
> resolution. You know, people don't realize how important human
> life is, what a precious gift God gives us. Life is so cheap to so
> many people. I wish everyone could see Edwarda and realize how
> important life is—how she is a fighter and how we've hung on to
> it. And the only way we could do it was with God as our part-
> ner...she has suffered three cardiac arrests, pneumonia, a collapsed
> kidney and lung. She was not expected to last a month...."

Edwarda is a miracle woman who survives, and who has gone from
a deep coma to a state that is like coming out of a deep sleep where
she can hear people around her, but can't break through.

Edwarda's room is decorated with pictures and objects that reflect
the spiritual awareness that I have described. There are pictures of
Jesus Christ, the Virgin Mary, medals, relics, statuettes, and healing
lights. An Infant of Prague statue sits on the window sill above
Edwarda's bed. During World War I, a nun kept 350 names of soldiers
under the statue. Every single one came home safely. Edwarda's name
has been at the statue's feet for over 25 years. The Bible is next to her
bed, and she receives Holy Communion through the catheter that
feeds her. Regular masses and prayers are said for her in her room,
also.

The Blessed Mother occupies the place of greatest distinction. I ask
you to suspend disbelief as you read about the entrance of the Blessed
Mother into this story. You will read about Mary explaining to Kaye that
Edwarda's comatose state is a part of the choice that Edwarda made as
a young girl to fulfill her own spiritual destiny. Edwarda's silence and
immobility befuddle our intellect, but I think you will agree, as you
read the Blessed Mother's explanation, that there is a God force present that resonates perfectly with our spirits.

After 22 years of caring for her daughter, Kaye was accustomed to
walking into Edwarda's bedroom from the kitchen, where she prepared
food every two hours. In the fall of 1992, she was astounded by what
she encountered. Here is Kaye's description of what happened:

I leave the small light on in her bedroom, and I leave the television on so that there's a light so I don't trip when I go in with food. I noticed when I started up the hall that the light was off. And I thought, Oh, darn, the bulb blew.

Well, when I stepped into the room, I looked, and the television was not on, but there was such bright light in that room. I thought I surely wasn't so sleepy that I turned the fluorescent lights on when I left. But what I saw wasn't fluorescent. It was something standing by my door. And I thought someone got in the door, and they were going to hurt Edwarda. I couldn't talk. All I saw was this person standing there.

I asked Kaye what the person looked like.

At that time, I couldn't figure out what it looked like. All I saw was—well, I was so startled and so scared because we'd been robbed so many times, and I thought someone had gotten in here. I sat on the chair and just looked at it. Then it said something, and I asked who it was. I didn't say another word. I didn't know how long I sat there. I thought it was hours. It was Edwarda's 4:00 A.M. feeding, and when I looked at the clock after she left, it was ten after 4:00. The person had been standing there for ten minutes, and I still couldn't talk. I was scared.

Questions tumbled from my lips. "Was there a light? Did you feel an energy in the room? Did you feel peaceful, or did you feel thoroughly frightened?" I asked all at once.

Kaye replied, "I didn't feel anything. I was so scared."

"Were you shaking?"

"I was shaking. I just put my hands on Edwarda so no one could take her," Kaye added.

"And where was this entity?" I asked.

"Right by my glass doors, right as you come in."

"Not by Edwarda?"

Kaye shook her head. "No, not by Edwarda. At the bottom of the bed, not the top. And it really scared me, and so I just sat there, but then I was going to hand her the food I had brought in, but the food was cold, so I got more. I thought maybe I was hallucinating, or maybe I'm crazy, or maybe I'm just dreaming. So I got her back to sleep. I fed her and just sat there holding her and watching the door so no one would come in or out.

"The next night when I came for her midnight feeding, the light was still on, and the TV was on, but you couldn't hear it. And here at the bed was this figure again."

"Did it have substance?" I asked. "Arms? Legs?" I really wanted to know.

"It had. It was standing. It looked like...exactly like the Sacred Heart of Mary picture I have. She said, 'Are you still scared?' I told her not as much. She told me not to be afraid of her, and I wasn't."

Kaye related more of the experience:

> When I asked her who she was, she wouldn't say. I asked her if she was an angel, and she smiled. I thought, Well, the guardian angel come down. When Edwarda was a kid, I used to tell her to move around and make room for her guardian angel. (I still move over so there's room when I get in the car.)
>
> She smiled and said, "This is a blessed child." When I agreed that Edwarda was blessed, she said, "No, this is a blessed child; she isn't just blessed." When I asked her what the difference was, she said, "She is a victim soul." I didn't know what that was and wanted to know if it was bad, and she said, "Oh, no, I never give bad tidings." I told her that I didn't think she would and that I don't let bad tidings come into Edwarda's room. She smiled, and I asked her how I could find out what a victim soul was. She told me to ask in the right places, and I would find out.
>
> She was holding Edwarda's forehead and invited me to pray with her. She wanted to know what my favorite prayer is, and I said it was the rosary. We said the complete rosary—she said the first half, and I said the second half, like a priest does. Then I begged her to tell me what a victim soul was because I felt so worried that I wouldn't be able to find out, and she said, "I'm not going to tell you. It will do you well to find out. Do not worry; it is not bad."

The next morning, Kaye began calling to find out the meaning of a *victim soul*.

> *I called several priests. I called ministers, too. I had two ministers in here an awful lot, but they didn't know, so I called a cardinal that I had been in contact with before, and he wanted to know who told me about victim souls. When I told him that something told me in my home, he wanted to know what I meant. I told him I didn't know, but I thought it was an angel, but I was hearing its voice and seeing something with my eyes.*
>
> *He started to laugh over the phone, and then he said, "It goes back to when there were martyrs." He said that some martyrs were called victim souls because when they had been asked if they would suffer, they had agreed to. He said he was puzzled because this was an obscure term that few have heard or used in modern times, and he wondered who had told me. The cardinal said that it could have only come from someone who had been present at the time.*

In doing my research, I found that a victim soul is a special kind of martyr. They are known in the Bible to have been asked by God to willingly suffer in order to revive His word in the hearts of His people. The important thing here is the idea that they have been asked. Taking on the role of victim soul is a choice that someone is given. The person has the right to refuse without incurring any wrath or punishment. Knowing what we do about Edwarda, it is hard to imagine her refusing.

Kaye continued describing what happened next:

> *Two days later, the Blessed Mother came back and asked me if I had found out what a victim soul was. I told her what I had found out and that I didn't know if it was correct. I then told her what I had learned from the cardinal, and she said, "Yes, that's right."*
>
> *I wanted to know what would happen if a person said no, and she explained that they would go on with their everyday mortal life, still working as they normally would do. So then I asked if Edwarda actually knew this and knew that she could say no. The Blessed Mother said, "Oh, everyone knows they can say no. That's in their heart." I then asked her to please tell me what Edwarda*

was suffering for, because I thought maybe I could hurry it up.

She said, "You can't hurry it up. She's suffering for it." I told her that I could take some of my daughter's suffering, but she told me that I was not dead and could not suffer for her.

"Did she talk out loud?" I asked Kaye.

"Yes, she did. Her voice is melodic, soft, not loud."

At one point, Kaye pleaded with the Blessed Mother to be allowed to take on some of Edwarda's suffering. Kaye explained:

I was really sick. My blood pressure was too high, and the Blessed Mother came to me and said, "You asked for it. Be careful what you pray for." All during this time, I'd sit down on the chair and fall asleep, but Edwarda was resting more peacefully than I had ever seen her.

During those six weeks, Edwarda did not suffer at all, but I couldn't take it, and I couldn't take care of her. I'd wake up, and my legs would not hold me. I stayed sick while Edwarda was peaceful.

I asked Kaye, "How did Edwarda's suffering stop, in what way, and how did you know?"

"Well, she went to sleep," Kaye explained. "She didn't cough or fuss, and I just knew."

It was obvious that this was not something that Kaye could take on and survive. This was Edwarda's choice to be a victim soul, according to what the Blessed Mother told Kaye, and no one could assume that burden.

I asked Kaye how she could be certain that this apparition who appeared in Edwarda's room was the Blessed Mother. Kaye related that she had asked repeatedly but could not get an answer. But something began happening that convinced her that this had to be the Blessed Mother. Kaye related:

She started displaying two different colors. Even though I am color blind, I could see something was dark, and something was light. And she was so beautiful, and her voice was so nice that she either had to be the best angel in heaven or the Blessed Mother.

One night, she said something about "My son, my son; you take care of this blessed one the way I cared for my son." She never calls Edwarda my daughter. She always refers to her as "this blessed one."

I asked Kaye again about the idea of a victim soul making the choice to suffer. "When you asked the Blessed Mother about a victim soul, she encouraged you to find out for yourself. You then asked her how this decision is made. Mary told you that the victim soul knows or agrees to take on the burden. Do you know if it is a conscious decision?" I queried.

"It is a conscious decision," Kaye responded.

"So Edwarda made a conscious decision?" I reiterated.

"She made it before she got sick."

"Just before, you think?"

"She made it right before she got sick."

I asked, "She never said anything to you about it?"

"She must have made it when we went to the hospital because she made it right before she fell into a coma," Kaye concluded.

I couldn't help asking, "From what you've since learned about a victim soul, does the victim come out of it, or do they die?"

"It depends," Kaye answered. "Sometimes when their suffering is over, they wake up. They have to work, to do something. I imagine victim souls took on this suffering until they freed the slaves."

"Did you ask the Blessed Mother what she meant when she said, 'It has to be known'?"

"Oh, yes," Kaye replied. "Before you even came, I had asked her, and she said this has to be known. That's why we were so happy when the Associated Press put it out, because it's been all over the country in different papers, by many different people."

Kaye went on:

But the Blessed Mother told me she would send a helper. Over the years, many people have come and said that they would do this or that, and then they would disappear. I think that's because they can't take the strain, or because they are afraid. If you only knew

how many times over the past 26 years people have told me they
were going to do this or that. Then you don't see them.

But then you came, and you said you would like to write a
book and have the royalties paid to Edwarda's Fund. You said to
ask the Blessed Mother, because this could bring a great deal of
publicity and people contacting me from all over the world. She
appeared that night, and when I asked her, she said, "I told you I
would send the right one. Yes, they are the right ones." (You and
your wife.) "They will know how to handle your situation, and they
will do it in a delicate way."

She said not to be afraid. I called you right away and told you.
I didn't want to bother you, but it's funny, I didn't mind bother-
ing you.

(Marcelene and I both feel that it is our honor to be able to produce
this book to "let it be known." As we all strive to feel more compassion
in our hearts, in some small way we are all a part of the story of
Edwarda and Kaye.)

I wondered if anyone else had seen the Blessed Mother and if Kaye
can see her when she wants to.

Kaye described an incident in response to my questions:

She comes in only when she chooses to. But one time, my for-
mer neighbor, Mary Anne, came over after the Blessed Mother
had visited the night before. Mary Anne asked me what kind of
light I had in the room. She called it an arc light and said she
wanted to get one for herself, after seeing it the night before. I told
her that I didn't have a light like she was describing. But she
insisted she'd seen it the previous night. I asked her to come and
show me, because I had no such light.

Well, she came in and went to the very place where the Blessed
Mother had been that night. There was no manmade light. She
must have seen the halo-like light of the Blessed Mother.

I asked Kaye to explain how she communicates with the Blessed
Mother.

"I've gotten over my awe of her," Kaye said. "I still revere her, don't get me wrong, but I talk to her as I would anyone. Others hear me talking, but don't hear her answering."

"So you talk out loud?" I asked.

"Oh, yeah, out loud. One day Laurie and John were here, and we were praying. Suddenly they saw me stop praying and start talking to something. I had lost sight of all else when the Blessed Mother appeared. After I finished talking, I started praying where I had left off."

"When she comes to you, do you feel anything else?" I wondered.

Kaye responded:

> It's real calm like a nice cool breeze. One time, my friend Mary came and heard me talking. She didn't hear anyone else, so she thought I was talking to Edwarda, and she came on into the room. She saw me intently holding a conversation, and she looked all around the room while I was conversing. For about 20 minutes, she said. She didn't know what was going on. When I realized she [Mary] was there, I asked her how long she'd been there.
>
> She said she'd been there for a while and wanted to know who brought me roses. I said I didn't have any roses in the house, but she insisted there was a strong fragrance of roses, and she went all over the house looking. [Kaye laughed.] She finally wanted to know what kind of carpet deodorizer I had. She wanted to get the same one.
>
> Some people smell the scent of roses from the Blessed Mother. Others don't. But no one else has seen her like I do, other than the light that I told you about with Mary Anne, our former neighbor.

Marcelene smelled the roses on several occasions when she entered Edwarda's room and commented to me about it. But I have only noticed the lightness of the energy in Edwarda's room and how peaceful I always feel when I enter that holy space.

"Kaye, do you ever ask the Blessed Mother, 'Why'? Why has my daughter stayed in the comatose state for so many years?"

"No, I never ask why. I figure she has already explained that to me, and I am at peace with it. I have asked her several times to please tell me what she is suffering for. She just smiles, saying Edwarda will tell me when she wakes up. But I am concerned that when she wakes up, she will forget everything. The Blessed Mother says, 'She will tell you a great journey.'"

"Kaye," I asked, "why do *you* think she is suffering?"

"I call it suffering because she is not getting the things she would have gotten at 17 and 18, like going to the high-school dance. Every mother wants to see her daughter get dressed up in a gown and go out to the dance," Kaye explained.

"Maybe that is suffering," I offered, "but my feeling is that she's not suffering in the way we think of suffering. That one woman on *Oprah* that was in the coma for two years. Remember that? She felt that she was being cradled by God."

"Yes," Kaye answered, "I see that, but I figure it's what she is missing."

"But it is only what her body is missing," I said.

"Yes, her soul's not missing anything," Kaye agreed. "It's the human side. So many people are benefiting from her that those human things don't seem to be as important as they once were to me. Many people have told me that when they get stressed, all they have to do is come and sit in the room with Edwarda. They say they get the calmest feeling just being there with her.

"But I think when the Blessed mother says 'suffering,' she means in a physical way. Edwarda missed out on all the dances and all those years, and she looked forward to going to dances, even when she was 16. She missed out on all that."

"Do you think it will matter to Edwarda?" I asked.

"I feel that she'll get them back," Kaye replied. "Knowing her, it won't matter."

Kaye then told me that six months before Edwarda got sick, she asked, "Mom, do you think God is mad at me?"

"Well, that's a crazy question," Kaye had replied. "Why would you even think that?"

Edwarda told her, "Well, I think God wants me to be a nun!"

"Well, honey," Kaye had explained to her daughter, "if God wanted you to be a nun, he would have given you the vocation to be a nun. He would help you with that decision. It's a vocation. You don't decide. It is what you are chosen for."

Kaye continued relating this incident to me. "Edwarda said that she had seen some of the girls go into the convent, and she felt maybe she should do the same, but she didn't want to leave us (her family), and she wanted to know if God was mad at her about the decision to go to Notre Dame. I told her God wasn't mad about her decision to be a teacher or a doctor and not to worry like that."

In some mysterious way, Edwarda had an inkling about her destiny—not on a conscious level, or even in the realm of the intellect, but in the heart space where inner truth is experienced.

One day, Kaye casually mentioned what is perhaps the most compelling thing that the Blessed Mother said to her. "The Blessed Mother says," Kaye told me, "that once it is known, and Edwarda wakes up, everyone will know that the world will have to have a lot of love, and nothing else."

From my perspective, looking back objectively over the years of Edwarda's life, both comatose and during her first 16 years, she has personified this vision. There was, and is, nothing but pure, unconditional love in Edwarda. Kaye is our living example of how to apply it on the physical level every day of life.

Perhaps Edwarda is playing a powerful role in the transformation of the world, teaching us by her silence and her suffering that we must find another way, the path of love. Some do it with daily devotion, others write music, teach school, or minister to the poor in the streets of Calcutta. This is Edwarda's way, and while we pause to consider her, our senses tell us that she is "sick," that she does not move, that her life is wasting away in silence.

But when we consult our hearts and look a little deeper into this story, we see that in peace and in silence and in choosing to suffer for others, the world can be transformed. In fact, it is a story that Christians all over the world replay every Easter—a victim soul taking on the ultimate sacrifice and suffering for the salvation of others.

Perhaps on a different scale, there are victim souls who do it in their own way. In a sense, that is not understood by those of us who are stuck in the worlds of cause and effect, sensory observation, and scientific data. However, it is a way that is far more powerful than anything we can ascertain with our sensory or scientific input.

Kaye has been reluctant to talk publicly about the visits of the Blessed Mother and the subject of a victim soul. She was initially afraid of the reaction of the priests, and she feared that a circus atmosphere might develop when this information becomes public. But, at this point, she has removed fear from her consciousness. She told me that she is no longer concerned with how she is perceived by others. But in the past, she has had cause to be afraid.

One evening, someone drove by and put three bullet holes into Kaye's living room after an anonymous caller told her that they were going to put Edwarda out of her misery. The holes are in her living room wall, and she was fearful for a long time that someone would come to hurt her angel, Edwarda. But that fear passed from her life.

Kaye feels, in her heart, that truth will prevail, and that it will also set everyone free, as is written in *The New Testament*. She can handle criticism, doubt, and naysayers, because she has learned not to internalize it. Kaye is uninterested in making herself right or anyone else wrong. She knows that the truth, as she has experienced it, is nothing to be afraid of, and that publicizing the story will in some way be fulfilling Edwarda's choice to take on the role of victim soul.

The most troubling aspect of this drama is the worry that Kaye has had to live with for so many years over her growing indebtedness. She is convinced that this was a large factor in her husband's early death. The strain of working two jobs, having no insurance, and watching debt increase was more than this fiscally responsible father and provider could handle. I asked Kaye if this was still a big worry for her.

"It was," she responded, "but then I asked the Blessed Mother about it, and she said to me, 'My son gave you a mind. You are sharp. Listen to it, and receive what is needed.'

"And that's why I've written recipes and had them done up in books. I've run raffles just about every year. It takes a lot of work, but I don't have any group coming and doing it for me. When Edwarda first got sick, I had about five teachers come down and help me with envelopes and that. Now, most everything is done by me."

Kaye has remained in debt, but her faith in the Blessed Mother and the goodness of humanity is where she places her thoughts:

> *The Blessed Mother said to me that everything will be fine. She never talks finances, just keeps telling me that I have a brain and that I am not dumb when I tell her I am dumb. The Blessed Mother has told me if I was truly dumb and didn't know how to*

*go about it, that would be something else. But she says I am doing
precisely what I need to do. I told her I felt like a beggar in the
Bible, and she said that it was fine that I was not ashamed to ask
for help, because I always give help.*

And "give help" is the greatest understatement that I could imagine for this heroic lady and her "victim soul" daughter. They personify
what higher awareness and spirituality truly mean. Their home is a
pleasant sanctuary, a holy temple of unconditional love. The ancient
Sufi saying, "If you don't have a temple in your heart, you'll never find
your heart in a temple," comes to mind when I enter their modest
home and bask in the light of love that is there.

In the heart of Kaye and in the heart of Edwarda, I see such a beautiful temple. I am quite certain that the Blessed Mother would concur.

Applying the Lessons of the Blessed Mother

The five key lessons that we can all learn and apply from this chapter on the Blessed Mother, from my perspective, include:

1. *The power of faith is incalculable.* If you have an inner knowing that cannot be shaken, regardless of how tragic the outer circumstances seem to be, you will gain the strength to handle all of the challenges of your life. By looking past what we see with our eyes, and perceive the grander purpose that is offered us with our minds, we can not only handle the difficult times, but we can begin to bless them and be thankful for all that we are gaining from these struggles.

2. *Divine guidance is available to us at all times.* It seems to me that the appearance of the Blessed Mother to the O'Bara family reinforces the idea that we are not alone. When we know who walks beside us at all times, and when we have this knowing go beyond a mere belief to a place where all doubt has been banished, we have the opportunity to see divine guidance reveal itself to us.

    The idea of guardian angels is not new by any means, but most of us think that those angels are only available to a select few. Your faith in divine guidance and that inner knowing can put you into conscious contact with guidance from beyond this physical world.

3. *There are other dimensions to life than the material world.* The Blessed Mother's visits reveal that there is much more to life than physical reality. There is a dimension of reality that transcends our senses. There is a life beyond the world of the changing. It is accessible to us unless we close the doors with our own limited perceptions.

    We must get quiet, and go within to gain access to these other spiritual dimensions. The force that allows it all to stay together is unconditional love. The more love you have for yourself and are willing to extend outward unconditionally, the more likely you are to know the power and bliss of the energy that is the Blessed Mother.

4. *The power of prayer is immense in providing us with strength.* Take time each day to pray, as Kaye has done throughout her long journey with Edwarda's silence. Give yourself the inner conviction that there is more to this experience than your mind tells you. The power of prayer is well documented in Larry Dossey's book, *Healing Words.* Even scientists are beginning to encourage prayer in the healing process. Kaye and Edwarda's story gives us fresh evidence that prayer creates peace during times that are perceived by our physical selves as tragic.

5. *We all have a purpose.* Perhaps the greatest lesson that is to be learned from the appearance of the Blessed Mother is the revelation concerning the victim soul. It reinforces the fact that we all have a heroic mission to accomplish on this journey, and that we have a choice to make about it as well.

    Edwarda is doing her work in her way. We may not all understand it or even like it, but nevertheless, it is in divine order. So too are you making a choice about your life each and every day. If you want to feel purposeful, then begin allowing the sacred part of you that wants you to be peaceful to triumph over the ego-mind that often keeps you in a state of turmoil and dis-ease.

This is the third of the three main characters in A *Promise Is a Promise.* The Blessed Mother continues to play a dominant role in both Kaye and Edwarda's daily lives.

In the fourth chapter, Marcelene will share with you, as the mother of seven children, her own unique perspective of her association with Kaye and her family. The fifth and final chapter is devoted to some of the miracles that have taken place around these three divine beings.

Edwarda as an infant

Colleen, Joe, and Edwarda in 1959

Edwarda (left), Prince, and
Colleen in 1958

Edwarda (right) and Colleen in 1958

Edwarda (right) and Colleen
as young girls

Edwarda in her dance-recital costume

Edwarda in her cap and gown

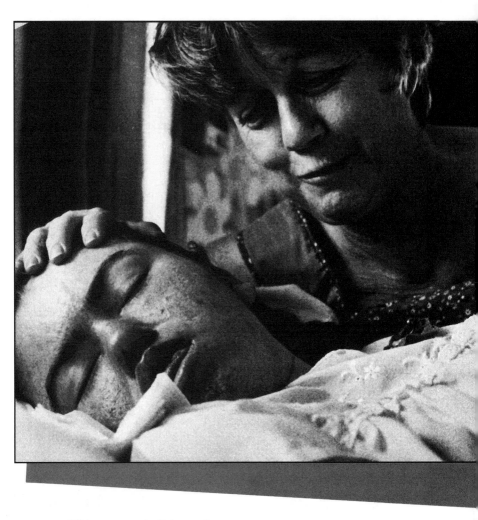

Kaye and Edwarda in 1979,
nine years into her coma

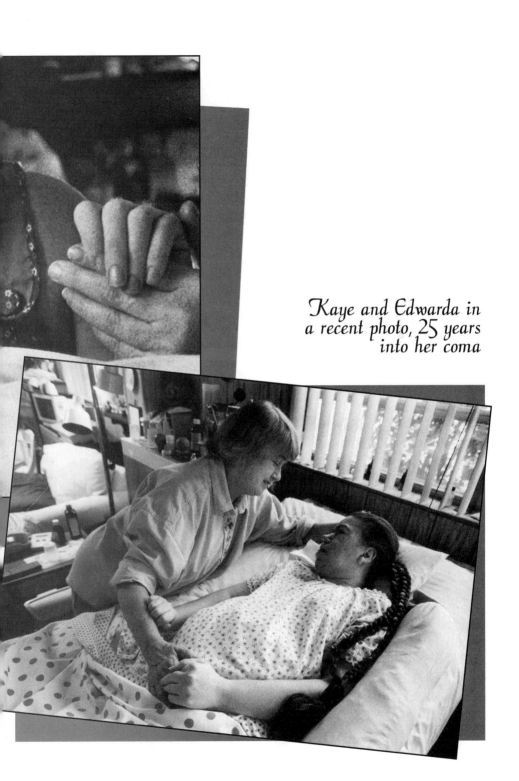

Kaye and Edwarda in a recent photo, 25 years into her coma

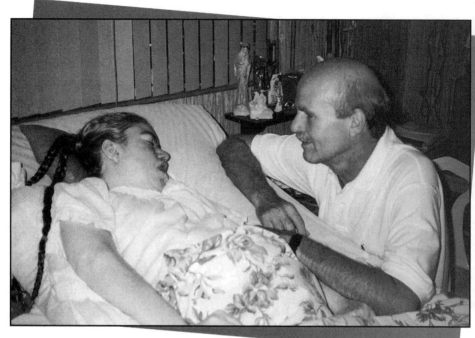

Edwarda and Wayne

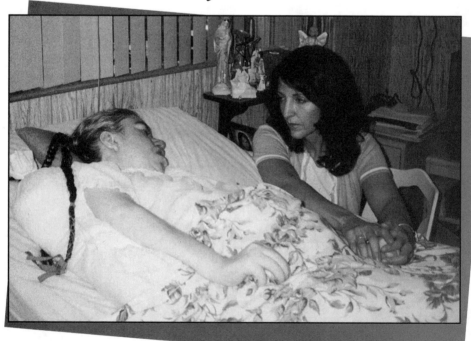

Edwarda and Marcelene

Edwarda,
Wayne,
and Kaye

Edwarda,
Colleen,
Wayne,
Kaye, and
Marcelene

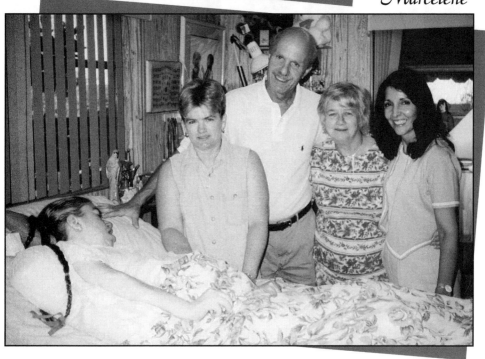

Chapter Four

A Mother's Point of View

(by Marcelene Dyer)

*"Be not ashamed, woman...You are the gates of the body,
and you are the gates of the soul."*
—Walt Whitman

I am Marcelene Dyer, the wife of Wayne Dyer—the love of my life and a man I greatly respect and admire. He so generously asked me to share my thoughts in this book, A *Promise Is a Promise.* I pray my words bring honor to him and the O'Baras. All are richly deserving.

Never have I seen Wayne so moved, so deeply interested, as he was the morning in December of 1995 when he gave me a newspaper article he had just read. It was a story about Kaye O'Bara and her comatose daughter, Edwarda.

Wayne was astounded by this story of a mother who, for the last 26 years, lovingly cared for her daughter who lay in a coma in her parents' bedroom. This care included feedings every two hours, around the clock. He said, "This woman wakes up every night in two-hour increments. That's been going on for over a quarter of a century. She must be a saint."

Once Wayne said to me, "I don't do enough. I don't do enough giving outside of our families. I have to start doing more." God may have been listening, because this man is today doing everything he can think of to help this family.

Arrangements were made for Wayne to meet the family, and he asked me to join him. I wasn't worried about seeing a woman, only a few years younger than myself, in a coma. I just kept thinking how sad for the family, and that the time element of 26 years was such a long time to be in that state. My own faith was quick to respond to these thoughts with the words: "God's will be done. God had special reasons." With these thoughts in mind, we arrived at the O'Bara home.

Meeting Kaye O'Bara was like a breath of fresh air. She is joy and laughter and love and wisdom tucked wonderfully inside her 68-year-old form. We brought her some gifts of food, and she was genuinely appreciative. Most of all, she was truly tickled to meet Wayne Dyer.

She told me she has written to sports figures, radio personalities, priests, mayors, lots of famous people, and even the President. Kaye confided, "It's funny, because I can write to anyone for help with Edwarda, but when I received the book *Real Magic* that he [Wayne] sent me, I couldn't write to him. I don't know why. My friends told me to call him, too.

"Finally, at the bottom of a thank-you letter that my niece Pam wrote, I invited him to come down to meet us. That's something I've never done before either. People call and say they're coming over, and I say all right, but you people are the first I've asked to visit us."

As Kaye was telling me this, I wondered if Wayne's desire to do more for others, and to help Kaye with her financial needs, was orchestrated by God. In my life, I've discovered that when I surrender my ego and allow God to use me, marvelous adventures of love and hope enter my world. This was to be one of those times.

Suddenly Kaye said, "Come! I want you to meed Edwarda." Down the hall we went into her bedroom. The television was on, and Edwarda was facing the screen. "I leave the TV on when I leave the room," Kaye explained, "in case she wakes up. I don't want her to think she's all alone." Then she turned off the set as we approached the hospital-like bed where Edwarda was lying.

As I got closer, I noticed a beautiful scent. It was lovely. Then I saw Edwarda's long, 20-inch braids tied with purple ribbons. As I walked to the side of the bed to see her face, I was surprised to see her eyes open. She was awake and very peaceful. I touched her arm and was so happy to feel such soft, smooth skin. She was so well cared for by Kaye.

I heard Kaye saying, "Edwarda, you have company. This is Dr. Wayne Dyer and his wife, Marcelene." To us, she said, "This is my baby,

Edwarda." Wayne and I said hello to her.

There was no sadness here. Nothing even close to it. There were get-well cards sitting on the window sills; gifts of rosaries and crosses adorned the shelves. Angel dolls and angel pins sat here and there. Framed photos of the family hung on the walls. Books and a stereo were in the room.

I asked Kaye where she slept, and she happily replied, "Right here beside Edwarda. I sleep here." It was a chair that opened to a narrow bed. So narrow, in fact, that she couldn't roll over or else she'd fall off. But this didn't phase Kaye. She was where she was needed—beside her daughter.

Oddly enough, Wayne and I both automatically spoke to Edwarda telepathically. I know I didn't even think about it. I simply began talking to her with my thoughts. I told Edwarda that I was honored to meet her and her mother. Edwarda was looking to my right. Then I began telepathically telling her that I received much joy from being the mother of seven children. Suddenly, Edwarda was looking deep into my eyes. Her stare was the most penetrating of any I have ever experienced. She saw me, I'm sure of it.

As I stepped back, I heard Wayne say to Kaye, "I feel she can see me. Tell me about her coma." He had felt a recognition, too.

Kaye told us that when Edwarda first went into the coma on January 3, 1970, it was very deep. Her eyes would not shut, her tongue thrust out of her mouth, and there were many serious, life-threatening emergencies in those first few months. Then she stabilized. Kaye believes Edwarda is at level nine now. She explained this would be parallel to where we are each morning when it is time to wake up, but we want to stay asleep.

I wondered if Kaye was saying that over the past 26 years, Edwarda is slowly getting closer to waking up. Kaye's response was emphatic: "I don't *think* she will wake up. I *know* she will." I looked into Kaye's eyes as she spoke and saw not a flicker of doubt. Her gaze was steady, sure.

This woman, Kaye O'Bara, is the epitome of love and spiritual practice. Her home is open to everyone, including strangers and many friends. As we sat and talked, I learned that Kaye and her deceased husband, Joe, were school teachers. Some of their former students, grown up now, still stop by to visit. Edwarda's childhood friends and their parents continue to visit and have remained close. Kaye's niece, Pam, teaches special-needs children and is the mother of two daughters. She is there every Wednesday to help out and have dinner with Kaye.

Edwarda's condition did not prevent Kaye from being a vital part of the world. The world simply began to show up on her doorstep. Priests, rabbis, and ministers call on the O'Baras. Once, while Wayne and I were there, Father Dennison arrived to say a blessing for the family. As he left, he said to me, "There's a holy presence in this house. I feel it every time I come to visit them." Kaye told me that several times religious leaders have said that they feel God's presence there even more so than in their own churches and temples.

I know what they mean. As I was saying good-bye to Edwarda at the end of our first visit, I began crying. Kaye warmly said, "Those better be tears of joy, not sadness." My emotions spilled over in response to the presence of love in that house, particularly in Edwarda's room. I recognized this profound feeling. It had happened to me once before.

Last year Wayne gave me and our daughters, Stephanie, Skye, and Sommer, the gift of a trip to Italy. We had a terrific time. Our plans included the city of Assisi. We visited St. Francis's small chapel, which is now completely housed inside a large cathedral to protect it.

When I walked inside his humble church, I was overcome with that same feeling. It engulfed me so completely that the infamous lump-in-the-throat could not be held, and the weeping began. Turning to find Wayne, I saw the same expression.

In Edwarda's room, especially, this feeling held me in love, and the tears washed down my face. I knew I was somewhere very special. I said, "Thank you," and was grateful.

During future visits, Kaye began telling us about her most beautiful visitor. Approximately four years ago, during the night, Kaye awoke to the alarm clock's reminder of the next two-hour feeding. The TV was on, without the sound, plus the lamp was left on to light Kaye's way down the hall to the kitchen.

Kaye prepared the formula that included the foods Edwarda most loved while she was growing up, plus some water and liquid vitamins. As she walked back down the hall, she saw that the light had gone out in the lamp. Entering the room, she noted that the TV was also off.

Odd, she thought, the room is well lit.

As she looked toward Edwarda's bed, she saw an apparition near the sliding-glass doors. Kaye sat down on the opposite side of Edwarda's bed and stared at this illumination. There was no sense of time. Then the vision disappeared. Kaye said to us, "At first I thought I was hallucinating. Maybe not sleeping for more than 2 hours at a time over these last 26 years finally took its toll on me." She told no one.

During the next visitation, Kaye knew that this was Mother Mary who was standing by Edwarda's bed. This time she spoke to Kaye. She asked Kaye if she was still afraid. Kaye said she was not. She asked Kaye if she knew who she was, and Kaye said she did. They communicated, and then Mother Mary disappeared. Kaye was honored and humbled beyond words.

I believe in my heart that Kaye is completely honest about this. I believe she has communicated with a holy being. Since our initial visit, Kaye has given me messages from Mother Mary. I don't know how else to receive these words except to believe that they came from heaven. No one else would know this information. Because of this, I have no doubts.

Kaye told us that when Edwarda got sick and fell into the coma, she did not ask God why. When her beloved husband, Joe, six years after Edwarda went into the coma, died at their kitchen table of heart failure, she did not ask why. Her only other child, Colleen, who was 18 months younger than Edwarda, lost her best friend and sister to the coma, then lost her father, to whom she was exceptionally close. And then Colleen lost herself. Kaye continued, still not demanding to know why.

Colleen, perhaps trying to escape all the pain, entered the world of drugs. She left home and spent some time living elsewhere. Kaye looked after Colleen's son, Ricky, who brings everyone much joy. Kay never asked why.

Then in 1982, Kaye had a massive heart attack. Her only vacation during these 26 years was her ten-day stay in the hospital. She didn't ask God why. Instead, she said, "I'm glad it happened to me and not someone else, because I can take it. I'm strong enough." That's faith. Faith we can all learn from. Faith that doesn't ask God for explanations. Faith that accepts what God presents, knowing that we are strong enough to carry the weight. Wayne and I are in awe and appreciation of the faith that Kaye symbolizes.

Each time as we drive home after visiting the O'Baras, Wayne and I share our feelings about the experience. Kaye and Edwarda have profoundly touched our lives forever.

Just as unique is Colleen, who has touched our hearts deeply as well. She is an extremely private person, yet she shared her life's drama with us one day, giving us permission to write what we felt was appropriate.

Colleen single-handedly pulled her life together, using her incredible courage and strength to stay drug free. She has been deeply wounded in this lifetime and will always be in my prayers. She has my admiration and my love.

Her son, Ricky, private like his mother, seems like a wonderful young man. I haven't gotten to know him yet, but I've seen him play a mean game of basketball in their driveway.

One Sunday, we decided to bring some of our children with us to visit. Kaye also loves children. She said she couldn't wait to meet them. Shane and Stephanie were working that day, helping to support themselves as they attend a university nearby. Sommer was horseback riding at the ranch she so loves. Wayne's daughter, Tracy, lives and works in Minnesota, so she wasn't available.

We brought Skye, age 14; Serena, age 10; Sands, age 8; and Saje, age 6, to visit the O'Bara family. On the way to their house, we spoke to them about Edwarda's diabetes and the blood tests that she requires each day. If her sugar is high, Kaye gives her an injection of insulin. We wanted the children to be prepared. We spoke of her coma, also. They asked questions, and we did our best to comfort them and allay their concerns.

Upon arrival at the O'Bara house, Kaye met us at the door and gave each child her complete attention during their introduction. I had taught the children to bring a small gift when they go to someone's home. Kaye excitedly thanked each of them for the food they brought. Then she ushered them in to meet Edwarda. Kaye introduced Skye, Serena, Sands, and Saje to her.

I stood quietly by our children as they looked at Edwarda. Skye and Serena silently wept. Sands remained his mellow self and seemed completely at ease with the situation. Saje stayed closest to me. Kaye told Skye and Serena that their tears better be tears of joy, too, and they smiled.

Sharing stories about Edwarda as a little girl who loved to dance and read stories about saints made her appealingly different. She had a collection of books on saints and spent hours in her room each day reading. Quite unusual, yet I couldn't help but feel Edwarda was preparing herself for her life on earth in the spirit world.

Serena taught us so clearly how naturally she adapted to her new friend. She stood silently by Edwarda's bed, placing her thumb between Edwarda's eyes on her forehead. She remained like that for several minutes. Serena began to rub Edwarda's head, and I had the sense that Serena was speaking with her. She stared into Edwarda's eyes for a long time. Walking back toward us, she said, "It's not necessary to use words to speak to her. I talked to her with my mind." Wayne and I knew she was explaining telepathy to us.

I was surprised by her knowledge. Yet, children begin communicating spirit to spirit as newborns. My own seven children could tell me what they wanted before crying was necessary. Consequently, I went to them before they spent their energy on tears.

As they grew up, I noticed that their descriptions of other children were rarely about physical appearance. Most of the time they would say something like, "You know, Mom, he's so nice." Or, "Mom, you will love her, she's so sweet and kind." They don't see the color of the hair, or eyes or skin. Nor do they see fat or thin, tall or short. It seems that this material vision has to be taught.

In my own family, my parents almost never gave me a compliment. I remember this well because the one time they said I looked very nice (I was going to a prom at my high school), I was shocked by their words. What a blessing for me to be as unconcerned about whether I felt I was beautiful or not.

When I fell in love at 15, my friends asked me what "he" looked like since he didn't go to our school. I couldn't tell them his eye color or hair color or even his height. They were aghast. I only knew I liked "him," not what I saw. It didn't even register.

So, that day, in the O'Bara home, my nonjudgmental daughters, Skye and Serena, were singing a song for Edwarda and Kaye. Skye sang,

"I Will Always Love You" so perfectly and purely. Serena sang, "I Enjoy Being a Girl" with such personality. I love to hear them sing. Sands spoke up and said he could play the piano. Then I heard little Saje, who was still standing against me, finally speak. She wanted them to know that she was taking piano lessons, too. It was all so natural.

We were standing at the side of a woman's bed while she lay in a body with the needs of a newborn. We were not talking to this body. We were singing, talking, and looking beyond this form to the soul. There we were connected. Whether her eyes were opened or closed, Edwarda was with us in spite of being in a coma.

The definition of the word *coma* suggests a state of deep unconsciousness. Sleep would be more of a natural, periodic suspension of consciousness. Kaye and her husband, Joe, were told that Edwarda slipped into a coma in the early morning hours of January 3, 1970. Was there ever a question that they would place their 16-year-old daughter in a nursing home? Never. She was always going to come home.

If a doctor ever mentioned that if this was his daughter he would have her cared for in an institutional facility, Kaye fired him. She would not tolerate that attitude around her child. Maybe her body was unconscious, but Kaye knew that her soul was alive and hearing everything.

Over the last 26 years, Kaye has kept Edwarda up to date on the music scene and shared television shows with her. Edwarda hears the rap, the rock, and the reggae. Kaye sits and talks to her and tells her funny stories. She sees her daughter's laughter, too.

I've been at their home on numerous visits now, and I've watched Kaye pick up Edwarda's hand, fold it over hers, and then place it against her face and under her chin. I've witnessed the depth of love that is there, unspoken and rare.

Kaye doesn't hold any resentment and shows no anger or sadness. Since Joe died, Kaye has single-handedly found a way to provide for her family. Although heavily in debt at all times, she manages to get by. To me, this is nothing short of miraculous, considering that her income and medical insurance disappeared long ago. She has, over the years, found a way to raise a little money.

Recently, our family and our best friends, Jeff and Bonnie Krich and their two children, attended an auction that Kaye put together. I could only imagine the amount of work that went into organizing such an event.

Pam, Kaye's niece, gives freely of her time, and for almost 20 years, Kaye has had a nurse's aide named Ethel come in a few days a week to help her with Edwarda. Kaye told us that on many of her days off, Ethel will show up just to help out. What a love she is, and she gives the best hugs! Because of Ethel, Kaye could attend the auction that night. Colleen and her son, Ricky, were there, too.

Many people came by and reached deep into their pockets to help the O'Baras. It was a warm and friendly evening. Kaye didn't care if she made a lot of money; she was so thrilled to see everyone together. Her joy was seeing all of her friends. It would be impossible to not love this family.

When Wayne heard of their financial situation, he said to me, so matter-of-factly, "I'm going to write a book about Kaye and Edwarda. All of the profits will go to Kaye. What do you think of that?"

I looked into the blue eyes of this dear, kind man, and I saw his resolve. I have personally seen him evolve over the years into that spiritual teacher we all love, and I saw this as his greatest act of serving yet. He would not only write this book, he would promote it worldwide and take nothing from it. All was a gift from him.

Was Kaye's unstoppable faith and love of life, no matter what has befallen her, to be rewarded? Was Wayne's need to do more for others being fulfilled? Isn't this the stuff of miracles?

As a woman and a mother, I understand about sacrifice. Particularly, it is the mother or the woman in a family who will be the one who takes care of and nurtures the baby or child. The ill person or invalid is almost always cared for by a woman. Not always, of course, but quite often.

Some would say it is our nature, our maternal side. We will be the last one to sit down, the last one to eat a meal, and the last one to rest—these are not so much the acts of a martyr, but rather, the truest way to show our love. Kaye is the epitome of this idea.

Kaye prepares the formula of the foods that Edwarda loved before she went into the coma. There are 12 feeding times each day. She sets the alarm clock at two-hour intervals throughout the night to make sure she doesn't sleep through a feeding. Kaye's body is compressed on one side—the side she stays on so she can see Edwarda. It has been over 26 years since Kaye has had an uninterrupted night's sleep. Could we even imagine that?

When Joe died, Kaye had to learn how to give injections and check Edwarda's blood-sugar levels throughout the day. Edwarda's throat must be suctioned because the swallowing reflex is asleep, too. Kaye bathes her daughter, dresses her, turns her often, and exercises her muscles with the physical-therapy exercises she's learned. Kaye is always thinking of her daughter's happiness. If a doctor is needed, she asks him or her to come to the house in regular clothes. Edwarda was afraid of hospitals and the doctors who worked there. Kaye doesn't want to upset Edwarda by having her see the all-white professional attire.

Edwarda's daily needs are carefully thought out and attended to by Kaye. She fills the needs of her daughter way beyond the physical care. She connects to her child's spirit. Therein lies the truth. Therein lies infinity. This is what I feel when I am in their home.

Oh, the material world is there, also—the "stuff." There's untidiness and clutter around. But it has no meaning, no voice. I could wear the same clothes at each visit. No one would notice. Kaye often has her false teeth in her shirt pocket; she doesn't care. The hairdo is just that—on her head. So what?

Kaye and Edwarda have traveled way beyond what most of us are caught up in, and they have experienced the bliss of being. A human being stripped of its cloaks. Glowing spirit. Singing of God, of love. There is a large, lacquered plaque hanging near Edwarda's bed. It says: "Where there is great love, there are always great miracles." It speaks to the healings that have taken place on many levels.

On one of those levels, I see myself as I climb back into our car after one of our visits. I have continually felt a calmness about my own life. Ongoing doubts or questions that I have seem to disappear. Wayne and I have acquired a new and holy closeness of great depth. Our priorities seem clearer, and our lives have more meaning. We feel that the O'Bara family has given us these personal gifts.

Edwarda is alive, not by artificial means. She breathes on her own. She may be one of the longest-living people in a coma alive today. As I stand by her bed, looking into her eyes, I see life, not emptiness. We are so simplistic to think that the outward signs of life, such as talking, walking, and doing are indications of living.

All of me that is alive—those inner feelings, my joys, my pains, my loves, my disappointments, my knowings, my brilliance, my weaknesses, are on the inside. Is it inside this body? Or is it inside my soul? A part of my spirit forever? Yes, that's what I believe. My spirit, the connection to the unseen world, houses the true me.

Edwarda is only in the spirit world today. She's our connection to it because, as our teacher—the very reason why I believe she is alive—we are guided to see her that way. She has taught me to once again look to the spirit of the person. To bypass all the trimmings. What does the soul whisper?

"A promise is a promise" are the last words that Kaye spoke to Edwarda as she asked her mother, "Mommy, you won't leave me, will you?"

Kaye said, "Never. I will never leave you. And a promise is a promise. If I can't keep it, I would say I'll try. I will never leave you, Edwarda. I promise you I will never leave you, baby. A promise is a promise." Quietly, Edwarda slipped into a coma.

Edwarda had a 43rd birthday on March 27, 1996. Kaye gave her a birthday party, as she's done each year. It's a lot of work. Over 50 people stopped by throughout the day. Why does she do it? Kaye said, "Edwarda loved a birthday party. I do it for her."

A mother's love. I understand.

Chapter Five

The Magic and the Miracles

"Her life makes our lives meaningful."

— Illiam Quinn, Catholic priest

The presence of the Blessed Mother has brought many changes into the household and lives of the participants in this incredible story. The vision that first appeared in the fall of 1991 brought a new sense of meaning into Kaye and Edwarda's continuing symbiotic relationship. The most significant thing that the Blessed Mother has brought to Kaye is an inner kind of knowing that there is much more going on here than appears on the surface.

To the casual observer, this is a story about a young girl who slipped into a diabetic coma in her 16th year, and who continues to be detached from the waking world of consciousness more than a quarter of a century later. It also is a medical story about a prognosis of almost utter hopelessness from the "scientific" viewpoint. And it is a story about a physician named Dr. Louis Chaykin, who has treated Edwarda all of these years without charging for his services. This, in itself, is something that many would call a miracle!

Finally, this appears to be the story of a mother foregoing her personal concerns, including her own health, while unconditionally loving and devoting herself to her comatose daughter for over a quarter of a century. Here is a mother doing virtually all of the work, including fund raising, to keep her daughter alive in her own home. Edwarda's survival has much to do with both Kaye's unconditional love and with her refusal to send Edwarda to a nursing home where her expenses would be covered. But the presence of the Blessed Mother in this epic makes the surface details only that—surface.

This story transcends the surface facts, and leads us to a world that is beyond what we observe with our senses. The Blessed Mother's entrance into Kaye's life that autumn night provided Kay with something that she had only surmised up until that point. It gave her something tangible to go with her incredible faith and undying love. Now, at last, Kaye felt there was a far greater purpose than she had known before her visit from the Blessed Mother and her newly acquired information about victim souls.

Kaye had been willing to follow her own instincts in Edwarda's care and survival for over two decades prior to the first visitation by the Blessed Mother. Now she felt she knew why. This brought peace to Kaye concerning everything about her life during the previous 21 years.

The Blessed Mother told her that the right people would show up in her life, that finances would be taken care of, that Edwarda was on a mission known only to her and to God, and that Kaye's actions were perfect in that she had demonstrated, despite the greatest of challenges, the divine love of God and His son.

In this final chapter, I will relate a few of the many miracles and some of the real magic that I associate with the involvement of the Blessed Mother with Kaye and Edwarda O'Bara. Kaye is certain that Edwarda chose to take on the burden of a victim soul. She doesn't know the reasons for her daughter's choice, or the length of time that this will endure. But her faith in the spiritual nature of this all-consuming event is unwavering.

One of the most astonishing stories occurred in the early months of 1995. Kaye spoke about it with a calm sense of its mystery and rightness:

> *Two Spanish-looking women knocked at my door one day, out of the blue. One of them asked me if I was Mrs. Edwarda, and could they come in. The other one just kept looking while I explained that I was Edwarda's mother and invited them in. The one woman said her name was Mary and that her companion was*

her sister, Anne. They wouldn't give me their last names and wanted to come in and pray with Edwarda.

I am very careful about anyone staying alone with Edwarda, but I had a good feeling about these two women, so I agreed when they asked if they could pray alone with her. I walked to the kitchen and then quietly looked in on them. When I went back and glanced in, Anne had her head on the bed, and she had Edwarda's hand on her head.

I asked Kaye how old these women were.

The one must have been about 50, and the other about 60. They didn't appear to be from this country, and I was confused about the way they were praying. I thought to myself, Well, people pray in all different ways, just let it go.

I went back into the room, and they were still praying with Edwarda's hand on Anne's head. As they left, I asked again if I could have their names, and they said no, but that they would be back. They only gave the names Mary and Anne, and they left.

"They didn't tell you how they found you?" I asked Kaye.

Kaye shook her head, saying, "No, they wouldn't tell me how they came or anything. Two days later, a man came to my door and said he needed to measure for the carpet. I told him that I hadn't ordered any new carpet, and he told me that Anne paid for it before she went back to Venezuela. That's how I found out she's from Venezuela.

"When I asked him what her last name was, he said he was not allowed to tell me her last name. He also said I would have to take the carpet she picked and said it was high quality and beautiful when I expressed concern that it might be a color I didn't like. We made arrangements for him to come and install it the next week."

"Did you need carpeting?" I asked.

"Oh, yes. The carpet was very bad, and it was cheap carpeting that someone had put in for me about 18 years ago. It almost had a white strip through it where people had walked. So the sister called me the following Friday after they put the carpeting down, and she asked about the carpeting and said she was flying in from Pensacola and would it be all right to visit. Of course I said it was okay."

"Did she come?" I inquired.

Kaye explained what happened next:

> Yes, she came. I thought when she asked to come here, she must have family here. When she arrived, she said she was going to spend the night. We presumed she meant to stay at a hotel, and my girlfriend Mary offered to drop her off about 8:00 P.M., but she surprised us by saying that she was staying here at my house.
>
> I explained to her that I really didn't have room; my grandson has one room and my daughter the other, and I stay right next to Edwarda. She said it was okay with her to sleep on a chair, and so she did. The next morning, I asked her right out to tell me how she got here.
>
> She told me that Anne, her sister, had a brain tumor and had been going to all of the shrines in South America and kept being told to go to Florida. So she came to Florida and went to three or four shrines and was repeatedly told to go to Miami. Then Mary, the sister from Pensacola, was sleeping one night and was instructed to go to Miami and find the lady that has the sick daughter.
>
> So, they just started out, with no idea who they were going to see. They drove all over downtown Miami and went into a church where everyone spoke Spanish, and they started asking if anyone knew who it is that sees the Blessed Mother in her dreams. Someone told them it might be a woman named Rosa who lived north of Miami in Hollywood, Florida.
>
> They asked if this Rosa has a daughter who is sick, who has been really sick for a very long time. They said that the vision told them that the woman who sees the Blessed Mother has a sick daughter. At the church, they were told that they must be referring to Kaye O'Bara and her daughter, Edwarda, but that I hadn't seen the Blessed Mother because that would have been in the news stories that had been written about Edwarda.

(Kaye had always refused to talk to the papers about the Blessed Mother for fear of public rejection or repudiation by the Church.)

The women got our address because they felt that Anne, the sister with cancer, was supposed to see me and Edwarda. That's how they got here. She told me that she had seen Edwarda several times in her dream, and I said I hoped she wasn't expecting a cure for her sister's cancer. I don't want people to come and touch Edwarda and think they'll get all better.

She said they weren't and that her sister was under the care of a team of doctors in South America. I realized that if she was terminal, she might die any day, and I asked her to please let me know how she is.

I later realized that Mary came and stayed at my house to make sure that the carpet she had ordered was installed correctly, so that the furniture they had also bought for us could be delivered. She wanted to make sure that everything was all right. Once she was sure, she left.

Before Mary left, Kaye told me that she once again asked her to keep her advised about her sister's health. Kaye subsequently received a stunning phone call, in response to her request. Kaye explained softly:

The sister called me and told me the most miraculous thing. She said the doctors couldn't find any signs of the tumor in her sister Anne's head. It was completely gone. I wanted to write to Anne in Venezuela, and asked her sister for the name and address. But she said this must remain absolutely private.

"It was strange. It really was," Kaye concluded.

These strangers, one from another country, had a vision of a sick daughter whose mother saw the Blessed Mother. All the information they had was that she was in Miami. They asked at churches throughout the area and were guided to Kaye and Edwarda's home, even thought Kaye had never publicly spoken about her visitations from the Blessed Mother. They then showed their gratitude by purchasing all new carpeting, which was badly needed, and a houseful of beautiful furniture.

A miracle? A coincidence? The work of Edwarda while silently suffering as a victim soul? You will have to decide that for yourself. I am reporting it to you exactly as it was described to me.

❧   ❧   ❧

Another dramatic story unfolded around Kaye's efforts to pay the ever-present bills. At one time, Kaye had 32 MasterCard and Visa Cards, borrowed to the maximum. She'd borrow from one card to pay off another. Kaye described the situation:

"All of the credit cards were in my name. Some had my initials. Some had Kaye, others Kathryn, and they let me have them. Also, I had to borrow on my house frequently. I've had third, fourth, and fifth mortgages. Before Edwarda got sick, we were always able to keep up with the expenses. Then when my husband died, the expenses and debts went beyond anything I could have imagined. Edwarda's hospitalization coverage was gone a month after the coma. That was all that the school system provided. So we borrowed. We borrowed on everything."

"So you were absolutely maxed out with the credit companies?" I asked.

Kaye nodded. "I didn't dare to go back to the banks anymore, so I started to look in the paper for money, and I found an ad that offered loans with no collateral required. I called the telephone number, and a man took all the information and sent me $6,000! It was an amazing amount. Actually, he had someone come out and deliver the money to me."

"Did you tell him what you needed it for?"

"Oh, he didn't care. He said it didn't matter. He was just in the business of lending money, and there would be a little interest. I should have realized then, but it wouldn't have mattered because I needed it, and I had to get it. Edwarda was home with us. She needed a bed, plus her drug store bills were way over, the credit card bills were way over, and everything had mushroomed on us. The man said that I should pay him $100 a month, and I said okay. So I paid him every month for 15 or so years. I started when Joe was still alive. Joe didn't even know what this guy was coming for."

"How would you pay him?" I wondered.

Kaye recalled:

> He would come to the door. I would give him money, and Joe thought that he was just coming from the bank. I paid him from 1972 until about 1986 or 1987, then I didn't hear from him. I thought, Well, I'm paid up. I'm all right. But I learned later that you never get paid up with those kinds of loans. I didn't realize this because they never give you a balance.
>
> So, I didn't hear anything from him for about three or four years, and one day a man came to the door, on a weekend, a Sunday. The next day was a holiday, and nobody was home but me. He wasn't the same man that had come to me before, and I thought it was someone coming to pray with Edwarda.
>
> Then he brought up the money I had borrowed. I told him I didn't ever borrow money from him and that I didn't remember ever seeing him. He said it wasn't for him, it was for the man in the Keys (Key West, Florida). "I'm his collector," he said. I said that I hadn't heard from him in years, and the man said that was because he's been in prison.
>
> Then he told me that the guy had been in prison for 15 years and that when you borrow from these people, your debt goes on and on. When I asked him what I owed, it was some crazy amount in the thousands of dollars. I told him I had already paid way more than that. He said that the first six years you paid only interest.
>
> The debt could be settled for $600 if it was paid that day, he told me. It was a holiday weekend, and I told him if he came back on Tuesday, I would have the money for him, but he insisted he could not go back to the Keys without it. He had to have something, he said, because the guy he was collecting for would get real mad if he didn't.

"Did he threaten you?" I asked.

"Oh, yes, he was definitely threatening. First he looked at me and then at the pair of scissors there. I wasn't going to take any chances on him beating me up or hurting Edwarda."

"So you thought the worst?"

"Yes," Kaye said firmly. "I told him to come back at 6:00 P.M., and I would have the money for him. I thought I would call everyone I knew, and somehow I would pay this guy off."

"Was he scruffy looking? A gangster type?"

"No. He looked like one of those guys you would see with Elliott Ness, a real gambler, a collector. Like an old bouncer, but he was very definitely serious."

"Can you remember what his exact words were?"

"He said to me, 'I can't go back without the money unless I do something.' Then he looked at those scissors. I looked at him, and he said, 'Those are nice scissors.' That's when I told him to give me until 6:00 P.M., and he said, 'Okay, I'll come back at six.'"

"So what did you do? You had no money."

Kaye explained:

> Before he left, I asked him if I could give him a check that I knew would be guaranteed by a neighbor, but he wouldn't take a check. He seemed to feel bad for me, but worse for himself. He told me that he had a wife and children and that if he didn't come back with the money, his family would be harmed. I tried to get the phone number of the man who wanted the money to tell him not to harm this man's family, but he said he couldn't dare do that, and he left.
>
> No one was home because it was a holiday weekend, and I had no cash and no way to even raise it. Finally, I sat down in an old brown chair I had in there and said, "Come on, God, you always said you'd see me through. I don't care if you put a hole in my ceiling and I have to get a whole new roof. I need this money and I need it right now!" It was ten minutes before six, and I was still sitting and praying for the money to show up.
>
> I thought someone might just call me on the phone five minutes before six, but nothing was happening. Then I heard the doorbell ring and figured the guy was back a few minutes early and wondered what I was going to do.
>
> There was a little man at the door, a little Spanish man, and he said, "This is for you," as he handed me an envelope. I invited him to come in, but he said he couldn't, that he was just delivering the envelope.

Like I told you before, when people give me envelopes, I never look in, I just put it in my pocket and give thanks for whatever it is. I asked again if he was sure he wouldn't come in, and he said he was sure. He had to leave.

I went back and sat in the brown chair again and decided to look in the envelope, expecting 50 or so dollars, and maybe the collector would accept it as partial payment. When I looked, there were six new $100 bills, exactly the amount I needed.

I jumped up and ran across the street to Anne's house. She was standing at the door, and I asked her to quick, tell me which way the man who was just at my door went. But she insisted that there had been no man at my door. She said she saw me at the door, and Abe was about to come over to see if there was something the matter.

She described me standing at the door, holding my hand out, but there was no one there, and there was no car in front of my house. According to Anne, there hadn't been a car in front of my house for about three hours when that man left earlier. They had seen the collector and no one else. There had been no one and no car.

When the collector came and I gave him the money, he said he would be back. I told him not to ever come to my house again. I appreciated the loan and thanked him, but I said, "Money isn't going to do that man a bit of good. Nothing he does from this day on will ever help him. And that's just how I felt. That's the first time I was ever rude.

"How long ago was this? Do you remember?" I asked.

"Oh, that was in 1991, right before the Blessed Mother started to come. She came two months after that incident. I think she came because I was scared. That was the first time in my life I was scared. I wasn't scared for myself, but for my children. I think that's why the Blessed Mother started to come, because of that person coming to my house."

❧❧❧ ❧❧❧ ❧❧❧

How could there be a mystery person, who was invisible to the neighbors across the street? How does one explain that person's arrival while Kaye was deep in prayer over her plight? How could precisely that amount of money that Kaye needed, be in that envelope? How could Kaye's fear at the thought of the collector inflicting damage on her or Edwarda be taken care of so perfectly?

A miracle? Real magic? A coincidence? Are the answers contained in the appearance of the Blessed Mother, who assures Kaye that the right people will appear to take care of her and Edwarda? Are the answers related to Kaye's learning about victim souls and Edwarda's choice? Is a part of the answer found in the Blessed Mother's teachings to Kaye that God has given her the brains to handle this situation?

You will decide for yourself. Marcelene and I are convinced that part of the answer to this ongoing mystery has to do with people reading this book and participating in the compassionate act of including Edwarda and Kaye in their prayers, and helping them in any way that their heart dictates.

❦   ❦   ❦

Another mystery supports a conclusion that real magic is indeed part of the Edwarda story. Kaye explained that one day a man phoned from South Miami to tell her he had a rose bush for her:

> I asked him where he got it, but he said that he didn't know. He just knew it was for me. I was going to have him put it out back where my former neighbor had seen the Blessed Mother's aura, out by the mango tree. But then the Blessed Mother told me it was her rose bush, and it must be out front so people can see and enjoy its beauty, and she told me when Edwarda wakes up, she will go out and see all the roses and all the colors, and I can take a picture of her.
>
> Well, when he brought it up, it was small, and he said you have to do this and that to it. I didn't do anything to the bush, like fertilizer or whatever, just water. Everyone says you have to cut it back, tie it up, but I didn't do anything like that to it. Well, it's not my bush; it belongs to the Blessed Mother. If she wants me to

do something to it, she'll tell me. Well, it has grown and grown and grown. When it comes out, there are five different colors of roses on it: lavender, red, pink, white, and yellow. And, most amazing of all, there's not one thorn on the entire bush.

This reminded me of the story of St. Francis, who with his divine consciousness, could remove the thorns from the rose bushes in Assisi. My wife and I both examined the rose bush that was sent by the Blessed Mother, according to Kaye, and indeed, it has multicolored roses, no thorns, and it sits right in front of her home for any and all to see.

❧ ❧ ❧

During Hurricane Andrew, the financial difficulties that have been a part of Kaye's life erupted into a crisis. The storm sent a neighbor's shed through a window right next to Edwarda's bed. The gas-powered generator broke down in the middle of the night at the height of the 200-mile-per-hour windstorm that devastated a huge portion of South Florida. This generator is essential to Edwarda's life.

The suction device to remove saliva and keep her from choking is dependent on electricity. Electricity is also needed to prepare her formula and to operate her bed. The roof of the shed landed right next to Edwarda's bed, and there was shattered glass all over the room.

Kaye told me that she picked up shards of glass for over two months, but not one sliver ever touched Edwarda or her bed. The roof had to be replaced and, as Kaye put it, "The rain came in everyplace in the house, but it never rained one drop on Edwarda."

Kaye has been color blind all of her life. She says it was the Blessed Mother who corrected this situation completely. The Blessed Mother told her that she could now distinguish colors, whereas prior to this time, Kay could only distinguish light and dark. I tested her thoroughly, and she passed with flying *colors*! For Kaye, this qualifies as a miracle for which she thanks the Blessed Mother.

Kaye has told me many other stories of healings that have taken place in her life. One in particular stands out.

One of her former kindergarten students, from 30 years ago, began to come over and pray with her and Edwarda. This woman's name is Joy, and she has been tremendously helpful to the O'Baras for many years. I have met her, and she is a devoted care giver, and the mother of two children who have cystic fibrosis, which is a crippling disease with no known cure.

Kaye told me that she talked to the Blessed Mother on behalf of Joy and her children. "I said, dear Mother, could you please tell me something about my friend Joy, who fears that her children will be taken from her. I know children are only loaned to us for a short time, and she is such a good mother. Then the Blessed Mother stopped me and said, 'They are fine. They have been praying with me.' I told Joy what the Blessed Mother said, and she told the children, and they all were hugging and crying and feeling blessed."

Kaye told me that while they have not been totally cured, they have improved significantly, which is amazing because cystic fibrosis is generally a disease that gets progressively worse as children get older. Again, who is to know? A miracle? Real magic? A coincidence? A temporary respite? Kaye O'Bara knows for sure, and she speaks with conviction and honesty about her blessed visits with the Divine Mother.

❧ ❧ ❧

The final miraculous event that I want to relate concerns the artist's rendition of an angel on the cover of this book.

After hearing Edwarda's story, Christy Salinas, the cover designer, went to her studio and produced a cover in a matter of a few hours, which she submitted to the Vice President of Hay House, Mr. Reid Tracy. When she handed it in, Christy said, "This cover was channeled or something. I've never produced a cover so quickly or so effortlessly without even feeling personally involved. It seemed to simply flow through me."

I took the first rendition of this cover to Kaye to show her what the book jacket would look like, and she sent it to several of her friends and relatives in Johnstown, Pennsylvania. That evening, Kaye called Marcelene and told her that the angel on the cover looked exactly like Edwarda when she was a little girl. She also received two phone calls from people in Johnstown who knew Edwarda when she was a child.

Both callers wanted to know where that picture of Edwarda came from. They thought that it was a photograph, because it truly looked so very much like the child Edwarda had been.

When I told Christy about this, she was stunned because she'd had such an unusual experience when creating the cover. When I looked at old photographs, I could see how they looked almost identical to the artwork. After a conversation with Kaye, Christy kept saying, "I didn't do this cover. It just came through me."

⚜   ⚜   ⚜

There you have a short selection of stories, anecdotes, and personal accounts from those who have been touched by Edwarda and Kaye O'Bara in mysterious and miraculous ways. I am sure that you too agree that something beyond our own abilities to process with our senses is going on here in the O'Bara family. This is more than a tender story of love; it is a lesson for all of us. Those lessons have been enumerated at the end of each of the first three chapters. The final lessons are obvious.

First, it seems essential to know and to believe in miracles...to always remind ourselves that there is more to life than what we can experience with our senses...to recognize that other dimensions of reality are there for those who choose to enter, or for those who at least are unafraid to peer into them with an open mind and a loving heart.

Second, the idea of having guardian angels is something that more than three-fourths of the people on this planet believe, and yet most are afraid to announce these beliefs for fear of how they will be received.

Know that there is guidance available to us, and we do have angels to help and explain, if only we can open our minds to these wondrous helpers.

And finally, as Kaye has said to me so many times, "God never gives us more than we can handle."

This is a stunning story of unconditional love, compassion, commitment, faith, divine intervention, and care giving. There is much to ponder here. The idea of a victim soul may sound almost cruel, but who are we to doubt that each soul has its own way of expressing its purpose.

While Edwarda rests, she is also silently doing her work. Her life and that of her heroic mother have impacted our lives in a multitude of blissful ways. They have taught us to be more loving and compassionate with each other and to extend that glow outward.

I trust that you have gained from knowing about these beautiful souls who live with their challenges in the most awesome of ways. Take the lessons that they offer, and extend them into your world. I assure you that you and those whom you interact with will be empowered by the impact of that unconditional love.

And when you think of Kaye, caring for Edwarda every two hours, every night, remember the words that she uttered to her frightened little girl back in 1970, and make an attempt to live up to them in your own life:

"A promise is a promise!"

God bless you!

Please do include Edwarda in your prayers. If you would like to contribute anything—even a dollar will help—you may make a tax-deductible contribution to the address below. Kaye has so far been able to acknowledge every contribution she has received with a letter of appreciation.

THE EDWARDA O'BARA FUND
P.O. Box 693482
Miami, FL 33269-3482

About the Authors

Dr. Wayne W. Dyer is an internationally renowned author and speaker in the field of self-development. He has written numerous bestselling books, has created a number of audios and videos, and has appeared on thousands of television and radio programs, including **The Today Show, The Tonight Show,** and **Oprah.**

Marcelene Dyer is the mother of seven children and is currently completing her first book on a spiritual approach to childbirth and infancy care.

We hope you enjoyed this Hay House book.
If you would like to receive a free catalog featuring
additional Hay House books and products, or if you would like
information about the Hay Foundation, please write or call:

Hay House, Inc.
P.O. Box 5100
Carlsbad, CA 92018-5100
(760) 431-7695 or **(800) 654-5126**
(760) 431-6948 (fax) or **(800) 650-5115 (fax)**
www.hayhouse.com

Published and distributed in Australia by:
Hay House Australia, Ltd. • 18/36 Ralph St. • Alexandria NSW 2015
• *Phone:* 612-9669-4299 • *Fax:* 612-9669-4144 • www.hayhouse.com.au

Published and distributed in the United Kingdom by:
Hay House UK, Ltd. • Unit 202, Canalot Studios •
222 Kensal Rd., London W10 5BN • *Phone:* 44-20-8962-1230
• *Fax:* 44-20-8962-1239 • www.hayhouse.co.uk

Published and distributed in the Republic of South Africa by:
Hay House SA (Pty), Ltd., P.O. Box 990, Witkoppen 2068
• *Phone/Fax:* 2711-7012233 • orders@psdprom.co.za

Distributed in Canada by:
Raincoast • 9050 Shaughnessy St., Vancouver, B.C. V6P 6E5 •
Phone: (604) 323-7100 • *Fax:* (604) 323-2600

Sign up via the Hay House USA Website to receive the Hay House online
newsletter and stay informed about what's going on with your favorite authors.
You'll receive bimonthly announcements about: Discounts and Offers,
Special Events, Product Highlights, Free Excerpts, Giveaways, and more!